First Print Edition [1.0] -1437h. (2016 c.e.)

Copyright © 1437 H./2016 C.E.
Taalib al-Ilm Educational Resources

http://taalib.com
Learn Islaam, Live Islaam.ˢᴹ

All rights reserved, this publication may be not reproduced, stored in a retrieval system, or transmitted in any form or by any means, electronic, mechanical, photocopying, recording, scanning, or otherwise, except with the prior written permission of the Publisher.

Requests to the Publisher for permission should be addressed to the Permissions Department, Taalib al-Ilm Educational Resources by e-mail: **service@taalib.com**.

Taalib al-Ilm Education Resources products are made available through distributors worldwide. To view a list of current distributors in your region, or information about our distributor/referral program please visit our website. Discounts on bulk quantities of our products are available to community groups, religious institutions, and other not-for-profit entities, inshAllaah. For details and discount information, contact the special sales department by e-mail: **service@taalib.com**.

The publisher requests that any corrections regarding translations or knowledge based issues, be sent to us at: **service@taalib.com**. Readers should note that internet web sites offered as citations and/or sources for further information may have changed or no longer be available between the time this was written and when it is read. We publish a variety of full text and free preview edition electronic ebook formats. Some content that appears in print may not be available in electronic book versions.

ISBN EAN-13:   978-1-938117-28-2   [Soft cover Print Edition]

From the Publisher

GOLDEN WORDS UPON GOLDEN WORDS...FOR EVERY MUSLIM.

"Imaam al-Barbahaaree, may Allaah have mercy upon him said:

May Allaah have mercy upon you! Examine carefully the speech of everyone you hear from in your time particularly. So do not act in haste and do not enter into anything from it until you ask and see: Did any of the Companions of the Prophet, may Allaah's praise and salutations be upon him, speak about it, or did any of the scholars? So if you find a narration from them about it, cling to it, do not go beyond it for anything and do not give precedence to anything over it and thus fall into the Fire.

Explanation by Sheikh Saaleh al-Fauzaan, may Allaah preserve him:

'Do not be hasty in accepting as correct what you may hear from the people especially in these later times. As now there are many who speak about so many various matters, issuing rulings and ascribing to themselves both knowledge and the right to speak. This is especially the case after the emergence and spread of new modern day media technologies.

Such that everyone now can speak and bring forth that which is in truth worthless; by this meaning words of no true value - speaking about whatever they wish in the name of knowledge and in the name of the religion of Islaam. It has even reached the point that you find the people of misguidance and the members of the various groups of misguidance and deviance from the religion speaking as well. Such individuals have now become those who speak in the name of the religion of Islaam through means such as the various satellite television channels. Therefore be very cautious!

It is upon you oh Muslim, and upon you oh student of knowledge individually, to verify matters and not rush to embrace everything and anything you may hear. It is upon you to verify the truth of what you hear, asking, 'Who else also makes this same statement or claim?', 'Where did this thought or concept originate or come from?', 'Who is its reference or source authority?'. Asking what are the evidences which support it from within the Book and the Sunnah? And inquiring where has the individual who is putting this forth studied and taken his knowledge from? From who has he studied the knowledge of Islaam?

Each of these matters requires verification through inquiry and investigation, especially in the present age and time. As it is not every speaker who should rightly be considered a source of knowledge, even if he is well spoken and eloquent, and can manipulate words captivating his listeners. Do not be taken in and accept him until you are aware of the degree and scope of what he possesses of knowledge and understanding. As perhaps someone's words may be few, but possess true understanding, and perhaps another will have a great deal of speech yet he is actually ignorant to such a degree that he doesn't actually posses anything of true understanding. Rather he only has the ability to enchant with his speech so that the people are deceived. Yet he puts forth the perception that he is a scholar, that he is someone of true understanding and comprehension, that he is a capable thinker, and so forth. Through such means and ways he is able to deceive and beguile the people, taking them away from the way of truth.

Therefore what is to be given true consideration is not the amount of the speech put forth or that one can extensively discuss a subject. Rather the criterion that is to be given consideration is what that speech contains within it of sound authentic knowledge, what it contains of the established and transmitted principles of Islaam. As perhaps a short or brief statement which is connected to or has a foundation in the established principles can be of greater benefit than a great deal of speech which simply rambles on, and through hearing you don't actually receive very much benefit from.

This is the reality which is present in our time; one sees a tremendous amount of speech which only possesses within it a small amount of actual knowledge. We see the presence of many speakers yet few people of true understanding and comprehension.' "

[The eminent major scholar Sheikh Saaleh al-Fauzaan, may Allaah preserve him- 'A Valued Gift for the Reader Of Comments Upon the Book Sharh as-Sunnah', page 102-103]

This pocket edition is based upon appendixes taken from the larger book:

30 Days of Guidance: Learning Fundamental Principles of Islaam

A Short Journey Within the Work al-Ibaanah al-Sughrah With

Sheikh 'Abdul-'Azeez Ibn 'Abdullah ar-Raajihee

The role of Islaam in today's world is something which is indisputable. Yet there are many different understanding of Islaam from range from dangerous extremism all the way to dangerous laxity which nullifies most beliefs and practices of revealed guidance.

For every Muslim who wishes to live their life in a way pleasing to Allaah it is essential that they ensure that their beliefs and practices actually have evidence and support from within the sources of Islaam.

The larger work, which this smaller book comes from, approaches this challenge in a way that allows an individual to proceed through discussions related to this- a day at a time over thirty days- based upon the explanation of one of today's steadfast noble scholars.

Collected and Translated
by Abu Sukhailah Khalil Ibn-Abelahyi al-Amreekee

[Available: **Now**¦ pages: **370+**
price: (Soft cover) **$25**
(Hard cover) **$35**
(eBook) **$9.99**]

A CONCISE COLLECTION OF SHAREE'AH ADVICES & GUIDANCE (1): MISGUIDED IDEOLOGIES, METHODOLOGIES, & MUSLIM GROUPS

Translated & Compiled By
Abu Sukhailah Khalil Ibn-Abelahyi al-Amreekee

Table of Contents

Compiler's Introduction	*10*
(1) Leaving The Straight Path Occurs In Two Ways	*14*
(2) Concise Descriptions Of Twenty Seven Modern & Historical Sects/Groups/Religions/Ideologies of Misguidance	*20*
(3) Warning Away From The One Upon Innovation Even If He Does Good Works	*28*
(4) Ninety-nine Characteristics Of Various Misguided Groups	*38*
(5) It Is Not From The Way Of The First Three Generations To…"	*72*
(6) The Reality Of Secularism: "We Warn Against This Ideological Colonization…"	*86*

COMPILER'S INTRODUCTION

In the name of Allaah, The Most Gracious, The Most Merciful
Verily, all praise is due to Allaah, we praise Him, we seek His assistance and we ask for His forgiveness. We seek refuge in Him from the evils of our souls and the evils of our actions. Whoever Allaah guides, no one can lead him astray and whoever is caused to go astray, there is no one that can guide him. I bear witness that there is no deity worthy of worship except Allaah alone with no partners. And I bear witness that Muhammad is His worshipper and Messenger.

❁ *Oh you who believe, fear Allaah as He ought to be feared and do not die except while you are Muslims.* ❁ -(Surah Aal-'Imraan:102)

❁ *Oh mankind, fear Allaah who created you from a single soul and from that, He created its mate. And from them He brought forth many men and women. And fear Allaah to whom you demand your mutual rights. Verily, Allaah is an ever All-Watcher over you.* ❁ -(Surah an-Nisaa:1)

❁ *Oh you who believe, fear Allaah and speak a word that is truthful (and to the point) - He will rectify your deeds and forgive you your sins. And whoever obeys Allaah and His Messenger has achieved a great success.* ❁ -(Surah al-Ahzaab:70-71)

As for what follows:

The best speech is the book of Allaah, and the best guidance is the guidance of Muhammad, may Allaah's praise and His salutations be upon him. And the worst of affairs are newly invented matters in the religion, and every newly invented matter in an innovation, and every innovation is a going astray, and every going astray is in the Fire.

The noble Sheikh Muhammad 'Umar Bazmool, described accurately the situation we find ourselves in today as Muslims:

> *"A Muslim in our present age sees tremendous differing all around him among the Muslims, no matter in what direction he turns! Whether this is in the area of properly understanding the source texts of Islaam in different rulings in matters of ritual worship or in everyday dealings, or in relation to the correct methodology of calling the people to the religion, or any other issue! Such that among the Muslims there are those who just stand bewildered and confused in the face of all this differing. As upon every separate way there are those calling and inviting to it- making it attractive, legitimizing and justifying their way, yet disguising what they have of falsehood by holding up in front of it an element of the truth, such that it is almost impossible for the general people to distinguish what is correct!"* [1]

The esteemed guiding scholar Sheikh Saleeh as-Suhaymee, may Allaah preserve him, described some of the efforts and objectives of the people of misguidance in our age who are working to spread this confusion, saying:

> *"The enemies of Islaam diligently work to mislead people through their false understandings, and deceptive individuals, through spreading of multiple forms of corruption in regardless of whether this is the satellite television stations, or through newspapers and magazines, or through various other forms of media and propagation such as the internet and other technologies from the ways that are being used to spread misguidance and falsehood. All of this is put forward in the name of "freedom" in one instance, in the name of advocating "human right" in another, in the name of "women's rights and liberation",*

---
[1] Islaam Alaa Muftariq at-Turuq of Sheikh Muhammad Bazmool page 1.

in yet another time, in the name of "freedom and justice" a different time, in the name of "secularism" in another, and in the name of "progress and development" in different time. As well as other outward forms which they dress up and beautify in numerous corrupt coverings which they wish to spread and circulate.

However when looking at the results, these enemies began to despair of pulling the Muslims away from their religion, and when the majority, all praise is due to Allaah, the majority still remained upon the religion of truth despite these various campaigns and attacks, they then turned in favor of other a different path to accomplish their goals. This being the people of distortion and misinterpretation within the religion. Meaning those people who claim loudly to speak in the name of the religion of Islaam, where are in reality they are only working towards its destruction and assisting the enemies of this religion.

This is illustrated through the presence of many different movements and groups among which are, the sect of the Raafidhah, from them are those terrorists who adhere to those concepts previously held by the sect of the Khawaarij, from them are those numerous different paths of innovated traditional Sufism, from them is that recent movement calling to go forth in "dawah to Allaah" which in reality is under the dangerous leadership of certain Sufi groups originating in India, from them are those who cast forwards many serious misconceptions which leads and contributes to the eventual withdrawal and separation of people from the religion..." [2]

---

[2] From the lecture 'Crushing Statements Regarding the Reality of Modern Day Groups and Organizations' by Sheikh Saaleh Ibn Sa'd as-Suhaymee -given in the city of al-Qeesoomah

INTRODUCTION

This small work offers a brief overview and assessment from our scholars' view of many of the current ideologies and movements, which are present today outside of the realm of Islaam, as well as a more detailed discussion of characteristics of different misguided groups and movements within the Muslim Ummah, which Sheikh as-Suhaymee referred to. It also contains a more detailed scholastic discussion of the danger of secularism to the well being of Muslim societies.

The examination of the Muslim groups, organizations and movements is general and put forward in the light of the sources of the Book of Allaah and Sunnah as well as the beliefs and practices of the saved sect whose roots are the beliefs and practices of the Companions of the Prophet, may Allaah be pleased with them all. For a more detailed examination of two of the most prominent misguided groups please refer to the book, *A Summary of Observations by the People of Knowledge About Modern Groups & Individuals (1): The Muslim Brotherhood Organization & Jama'aat at-Tableegh*

I ask Allaah to make this work a means, among the many knowledge based aids available in our time, to help the Muslim men and women understand and practice Islaam properly as it was revealed to and then taught by our beloved Messenger Muhammad, may the praise and salutations of Allaah be upon him, his household, his Companions, and all those who walk upon their guidance until the Day of Reckoning.

Written by Abu Sukhailah
Khalil Ibn-Abelahyi al-Amreekee

(1)

LEAVING THE STRAIGHT PATH OCCURS IN TWO WAYS

All praise is due to Allaah. The author, Ibn Battah, stated, may Allaah the Most High have mercy upon him:

[Know, that leaving the straight way occurs in two ways:

As for the first of them, it is that an individual falls into error and strays from the straight way while he only intends good. Such a person is not followed in his error or mistake, as he is ruined.

Whereas the second of them is the one who willfully differs from the truth and opposes those who came before him who were steadfast upon guidance. Such a person is misguided and leading others to misguidance, a stubborn Shaytaan within this Muslim Ummah.

It is proper that the one who understands this person's state warns the people away from him and explains to them his condition of misguidance to them, otherwise someone else may fall into his innovation and thus also be ruined.]

Explanation of
Sheikh 'Abdul-'Azeez ar-Raajihee

[Know] meaning understand with certainty, *[that leaving the straight way occurs in two ways]* meaning that the one who deviates from the straight path and opposes the Sunnah is only one of the following two conditions: The first condition, *[an individual falls into error and strays from the straight way while he only intended good. Such a person is not followed in his error or mistake, as he is ruined.]* This category of person or the one in this condition he is the one that only desired and intended to do good yet even then he is not to be followed in his mistake or error, as indeed this error led him to being ruined.

Meaning that despite not having the intention to turn away from the truth, still he ended up opposing it. This person should not be followed in that matter even if they happen to be from among the Companions of the Prophet, may the praise and salutations of Allaah be upon him, or those who followed the Companions, may Allaah be pleased with them all.

As for the statement of the author may Allaah have mercy upon him, *[...as he is ruined.]* Then in relation to this there is a more detailed explanation and specified ruling needed. If this instance of opposing the truth came from one of the scholars with the scholastic ability to form independent Sharee'ah judgments based upon the evidences, and this error was a result or an instance of this scholastic striving to reach the truth, then despite the mistake he is rewarded for his effort to reach the truth, and he is forgiven for his result being an error or mistake. However we do not follow or adhere to them in that mistake. For the scholar who lived before us we continue to ask for mercy for him, since we continue to be aware that he slipped when he opposed a source text. This is what is correct even if the one who made the error was one of the noble Companions of the Prophet....

....Additionally, the authors' statement, may Allaah have mercy upon him, *[....as he is ruined.]*, also requires another detailed explanation. Again, if the one who is mistaken was someone who intended to turn away from the truth, then surely he is ruined. But as for the one who fell into error while striving to reach the correct conclusion, then this individual is not considered ruined.

About the second state, he mentioned:

[Whereas the second of them is the one who willfully differs from the truth and opposes those who came before him who were steadfast upon guidance. Such a person is misguided and leading others to misguidance, a stubborn Shaytaan within this Muslim Ummah.]

If he opposed the truth obstinately and turned away from the truth due to his desires, not simply as the result of a scholastic attempt to reach the truth, but simply due to knowingly choosing to instead follow his desires, then this one is clearly astray and leading others astray. He is considered a rebelling Shaytaan from within this Ummah. Yet this is the case if his errors and opposition to the truth are significant and reach the level of being major. Whereas if his opposition was only in something minor, then he does not reach the level of being given this description of being *[ruined.]*

Overall, we should see this general description by the author, may Allaah have mercy upon him, as an example or reflection of his strength and vigor, and in light of his severity against the people of innovation in Islaam, the strength of his efforts to defend the truth, and his diligence in warning from the people of innovation. However a further explanation of this mentioned description is required. There can be situations where an individual opposes what is correct within some of the fiqh issues of the practical implementation of the Sunnah. By this meaning issues such as the number of times that one raises your hands in the ritual prayeror what is correct regarding the short sitting after one's prostrations but done before standing up again in the ritual prayer, and other issues from those matters in which there is clear differing regarding them.

The one who differed in these specific types of issues does not merit having this description applied even if he is incorrect. As in some cases someone could oppose what is considered correct from the authentic Sunnah and yet not merit being described with this description of being *[ruined]*. But if someone opposes the truth in a clear matter in which their opposition in openly practicing it negatively influences others, then this person is misguided and misguiding others, and in this case this description as ruined is clearly valid and applied.

Overall, it is an obligation upon the individual that he warn against innovation in the religion. that he warn against the people of innovation, and the people of misguidance. This is so that the people do not slip or fall into that innovation which would lead them to becoming ruined.

(2)

CONCISE DESCRIPTIONS OF TWENTY SEVEN MODERN & HISTORICAL SECTS/GROUPS/RELIGIONS/IDEOLOGIES OF MISGUIDANCE

The following brief descriptions and definitions were mentioned by Sheikh Zayd Ibn Muhammad al-Madkhalee, may Allaah have mercy upon him, [1]

In the name of Allaah, the Most Gracious, the Most Merciful

1. **al-Wathaneeyah:** Pagans whose beliefs and practices manifest themselves in the worship of something other than Allaah, or who worship aspects of His natural creation alongside His worship. This is the association of others with Allaah in worship that Allaah does not forgive.

2. **al-Yahoodeeyah & an-Nasraaneeyah** -Jews and Christians, from among them are people from the Christians, who believe in the Trinity, those regarding whom Allaah said: *Surely, disbelievers are those who said: "Allaah is the third of the three (in a Trinity)....*-(Surah Al-Ma'idah:73)

3. **al-Hulooleeyah:** Those who believe that Allaah is present in every place. Yet Allaah, the High and Mighty is exalted and far above their claim.

4. **al-Itihaadeyyah:** Those who claim that there is an all encompassing unity of all things, meaning there is no difference between the Creator and His creation. Just as one of the misguided, may Allaah destroy him, said:

There is not a dog nor a pig
  yet it is one with our Allaah,

and there is no Allaah except He
  is one with the Monk in his monastery.

---

[1] As narrated on page 128 the book 'al-Ajweebah al-Athareeyah'

5. **al-Jahmeeyah:** Those from that sect who deny any that there is any true meaning or reality to Allaah's names and attributes. They deny what is narrated directly within the texts of the Qur'aan and Sunnah.

6. **al-Mashabehah:** Those who attribute characteristics and attributes of the single Creator to the creation, such as the Christians. Those who attribute characteristics of the creation to the creator from those sects that have proceeded upon innovation within the boundaries of Islaam. These sects affirm characteristics which are specific to the creation in its weak and deficient nature for the Creator.

7. **al-Qadareeyah:** Those from that sect who deny Allaah's decree. They say Allaah did not create good and evil, and some of them assert that Allaah created good but He did not create evil.

8. **al-Jabareeyah:** Those from that sect who state that human beings are compelled when they commit evil actions, just as a tree is compelled to bend due to the force of a strong wind against it.

9. **al-Murji'ah:** A sect of which there are of different groupings and levels. From them are those that falsely say when someone has faith or *emaan* then no sins or transgressions harm or reduce that faith, just as they say for the one upon disbelief that he is not benefited by any action of obedience. From them is a group that says *emaan* or faith is only a comprehension or understanding that one holds in his heart. From them are those that say *emaan* or faith is only a statement that you pronounce with your tongue. And from them is a group that removes actions from the boundaries of *emaan* or faith, or considers actions not an essential required part of *emaan* or faith.

10. **al-Mu'tazilah:** Those from that sect who assert that the Qur'aan is a created thing. They also claim that those Muslims who worship Allaah alone yet commit sins and transgressions may remain in Hellfire forever if they have not repented for the transgressions they committed before dying.

11. **al-Khawaarij:** Those from that sect who are upon the methodology of declaring people as disbelievers, outside of the evidenced guidelines of the Sharee'ah. They assert that anyone who commits a major sin or transgression even if they are from those who worship Allaah from the Muslims, then they have committed an act of disbelief in Islaam and that the ruling of such a person is that they will remain in the Hellfire forever if they die without repenting from that.

12. **al-Ashaa'areeyah, al-Kullabeeyah, & al-Maaturedeyyah:** Those from those sects who are people who have opposed the well-known scholars of the Sunnah and the Jamaa'ah in the area of the proper understanding of Allaah's names and attributes, and in the area of faith and what it is comprised of, as well as other areas of Sharee'ah knowledge.

13. **ar-Raafidhah:** Those from that sect who have opposed the guided Muslims in every area of their revealed religion both generally and specifically.

14. **as-Sufeeyah:** Those among whom there are ones who are extreme in their misguidance and innovation and other Sufees who below that in their opposition to what is correct from the Book and the Sunnah. Those that are extreme from amongst them affirm the concept of the unity of the Creator with His creation. Meaning by this that there is no distinction between the Creator and what is created. Such extremists are those who follow the thoughts and concepts of Ibn Arabee, Ibn Saba'een, and other astray individuals.

15. **al-Mufawwidhah:** They are those who state that knowledge of the actual meaning of the attributes of Allaah are delegated to or only known to Allaah. Regarding this group of people Ibn Taymeeyah, may Allaah have mercy upon him said, "*This is the most evil type of atheism.*"

16. **al-Waaqafeeyah:** Those who falsely state: We do not say about the Qur'aan that is it created nor do we say that it is not created, we abstain from taking a position.

17. **al-Baataneeyah:** These are people who are from those who are astray disbelievers, as they do not believe in the resurrection or that we will be recompensed for our deeds good or bad (due to their claiming that all revealed texts have a second symbolical true meaning as opposed to the apparent meaning of a verse or hadeeth).

18. **al-Qaraametah:** This is a specific sect is one of the branches al-Baataneeyah

19. **al-'Almaaneeyah:** Secularists, those who believe and advocate that religion should be separated from our lives. They consider religious practice as something which misguides and deludes humanity.

20. **al-Maasooneeyah:** Freemasonry, it is the worst group of those destructive fraternal membership organized associations that are used to serve the interests of the Jewish state and Zionists.

21. **al-Wujoodeeyah-** Existentialism is an philosophical thought which denies the existence of a Lord and Creator, just as it also rejects the sending of infallible messengers and the Resurrection leading to humanity's reckoning and judgement.

22. **al-Babeeyah:** Baabism is a religious movement that disbelieves in everything which the Messenger of Allaah, may the praise and salutations of Allaah be upon him, brought.[2]

---

[2] Sheikh Ibn Baaz, may Allaah have mercy upon him, discussing the history of this invented religion of Baabism said "*This sect believes that "The Gate" refers to the ignorant Iranian individual who practiced Sufism named 'Ali Muhammad Rida al-Shiraazi....Their ultimate view was that the "Baab" or Gate was greater and higher in status than all the Messengers, and that what was revealed to him of religion was more complete and more perfect than any previous revelation or religion.*" - Majmu' Fataawa as-Sheikh 'Abd al-'Azeez ibn 'Abd-Allaah ibn Baaz, vol. 13- page 169

23. **al-Qaadeyaneeyah:** This is a religious movement founded by Ghulam Ahmad, a person of disbelief and *zanadeeqah*, meaning from those misguided disbelievers who despite professing Islaam stand upon significant innovation which is at the level of major disbelief in Islaam.

24. **al-Qawmeeyah:** Nationalism an ideology which was found in the period before the coming of Islaam among Arabs. They do not differentiate between those who believe and those who disbelieve in terms of whom they ally with and support.

25. **ar-Raasmaleeyah:** Capitalism: it is an economic ideology that disregards the guidance of the religion of Islaam, and gives no importance to that threat of punishment for one's wrong beliefs and actions that Allaah has informed us of.

26. **al-Ishtiraakeyyah:** Socialism, an economic ideology that rejects the guidance of the Book of Allaah and the Sunnah, and judges and determines what is beneficial and good according to the people desires.

27. **al-Hadaathah:** Modernism is a philosophical movement. The worst of its malignant misguidance is the rejection of the fundamental beliefs of Islaam. They strive to distort the truth of Islaam, deceiving the people so as to convince them to abandon the religion of Islaam.

(3)

WARNING AWAY FROM THE ONE UPON INNOVATION EVEN IF HE DOES GOOD WORKS

heikh Muhammad Ibn Saaleh al-'Utheimeen, may Allaah have mercy upon, was asked,[1]

Question: There is a man who follows a specific Sufee order from the different paths or orders of the Sufees, he believes Sufism is a valid form of Islaam and engages in some of the innovated practices related to this. However, he is also a person who assists and helps in establishing some beneficial efforts for the general Muslims. So for example, if this man's innovated practices are openly criticized and spoken about and this spreads between the people, he will then stop assisting some of the people engaged in good works and stop helping people involved in some beneficial endeavors. So what is your position about what should be done in this situation?

Answer: Is this person someone who influences others in what he calls people towards?

Questioner: Yes, sheikh, he invites to the innovated practices he is upon.

Sheikh: So in this case which is considered more significant or important, the poverty of the people who are being helped or the danger of the misguidance that he stands upon?

Questioner: That misguidance he is upon.

Sheikh: Yes, the misguidance is more important to consider. As such, if this individual calls to his innovation and is someone who has an influence upon people, it is obligatory to warn the people from him. Even if he stops doing the good he was previously doing, then he is the

[1]   Open Door Gatherings: No. 266, Question 7

one choosing to make that good impermissible for himself. But as for the case where he might be left to misguide the people, meaning that his acts of innovation are not exposed, just so that people can keep acquiring a dirham or two from what he possess, then this is not possible to accept at all.

He was also asked,[2]

Question: Esteemed sheikh, if there is a person regarding whom there have been made a number of evidenced knowledge based observations, whether they are in the area of beliefs or regarding other significant issues, yet in addition to these issues, he possesses significant good. As perhaps he is an eloquent writer, or he has a distinguished position with people, or we see that he has some capabilities in calling to good that no one else has, then what are the guidelines of working with him and benefiting from him in this situation?

Answer: If he is someone who openly shows and engages in some matter of innovation, then it is not proper for someone to work with him nor to show any hesitation and indecision regarding being clear about him. Because even if the first person is not affected and influenced by this criticized person, yet others will still be deceived by him. By this we mean that, due to this first person continuing to work with him the general people would then be fooled into falsely believing that what this innovator stands upon is the truth and is acceptable.

What is necessary is that a person not be someone who wavers and vacillates regarding the people of innovation in the religion, whether this is due to benefiting from them financially or in some matters of knowledge, due to what this wavering inevitably leads to for other people in their being deceived and misled by such individuals.

[2] Open Door Gatherings No. 58 Question 10

It Should Be Seen As The Giving Of Advice For The Sake Of Allaah

Question: Regarding speaking about the misguidance of people of innovation, for instance that someone may say, "These people misinterpret both the verses of the Qur'aan and hadeeth narrations." or that people say, "These individuals do such and such of blameworthy actions." are these kinds of statements considered impermissible backbiting if it is discussed between people who were seeking knowledge of Islaam? [3]

Answer: As for statements and discussions regarding the people of innovation and what they have of incorrect concepts, or aspects of their methodology which aren't sound, then this is from the giving of advice and is not to be considered impermissible backbiting. Rather it should be seen as the giving of advice for the sake of Allaah, His Book, His Messenger and to the Muslims.

Such that if we see someone who is an innovator who is spreading his innovated belief or practice, then it is upon us to clarify and make clear that he is an innovator in the religion of Islaam, so that the people are protected from being harmed by his evil. If we see an individual who has ideas and concepts that contradict what the early generations of Muslims proceeded upon, then it is upon us to explain and clarify these issues. In order that the Muslims generally are not deceived by that.

In addition, if we see an individual who is proceeding on a specific methodology that will lead to harmful consequences for the Muslims, then it is upon us to explain and clarify this. Again, this is done so the people

---
[3] Open Door Gatherings Number 120. Question 8

are protected from that individual's evil. This is something undertaken from the direction of offering advice for the sake of Allaah and His Messenger and to the leaders of the Muslims as well as their general people.

Moreover, this should be the case whether those statements regarding the people who have innovated in Islaam are put forth between students or spread in other more general settings. It is not considered impermissible backbiting. As long as it is the case that we continue to fear the spreading of this innovation, or these false concepts, or the possible further spreading of this incorrect methodology which conflicts and opposes the methodology of the first three generations, then it remains an obligation upon us to explain this in order that the people are not deceived by these matters.

From The Corrupting Effects Of Innovating Matters Within Islaam

Sheikh Muhammad ibn Saaleh al-Utheimeen, may Allaah have mercy upon him, said, [4]

"Any individual who brings forth innovation in the religion, then we say to him, "certainly you who fallen into transgression and active wrongdoing which the Messenger of Allaah upon him be Allaah's praise and salutations, warned againsr in his statement *{Be warned against newly invented matters. As every newly invented matter is a religious innovation, and every religious innovation is misguidance.}* [5]

The following are some of the significant aspects of corruption from the corrupting effects of innovation in the religion. Firstly, it is a type of associating others in the worship of Allaah alone. Just as was mentioned by Allaah the Blessed and the Most High, *Or have they partners with Allaah (false gods), who have instituted for them a religion which Allaah has not allowed.*-(Surah Ash-Shuraa:21)

It is not hidden from anyone that major associating others with Allaah in worship is something which is not forgiven. As Allaah, the Most High, says, *Verily, Allaah forgives not that partners should be set up with him in worship, but He forgives except that (anything else) to whom He pleases...*-(Surah An-Nisa':48). What is also outwardly apparent from this noble verse is that associating others with Allaah is not forgiven even if it is minor.

---

[4] Open Door Gatherings Number 131, Question 5
[5] As narrated by Imaam Ahmad in his Musnad, Abu Dawood in his Sunan, and which Sheikh al-Albaanee has ruled is authentic.

From the corrupting effects of innovation in the religion: is that in practicing innovation a barrier or obstacle is put up to your preceding upon the true path of Allaah. Because an individual becomes occupied with that innovation, and turns away from true authentic confirmed forms of worship. Know that no people innovate an innovation the religion except that they lose what is equivalent to or similar to it from practices of the authentic Sunnah, or even a greater amount of what was truly from the Sunnah may be lost due to adopting that innovation.

From the corrupting effects of innovation in the religion, is that it understandably requires subtly maligning the Messenger of Allaah , may Allaah's praise and salutations be upon him. This is undoubtedly the case, as innovating requires believing that the Messenger of Allaah, may the praise and salutations of Allaah be upon him, either did not transmit and teach part of the guidance which he was sent with or that he was in fact ignorant and unaware of something which should be considered from the guidance of Islaam. A clear sign of the falseness of this claim is that regarding any new innovative belief or practice being attributed to Islaam, if we, for example, search for it in the texts of Qur'aan and the Sunnah but we do not find it, then either the Messenger of Allaah upon him be Allaah's praise and salutations, was unaware or ignorant of this matter which they consider part of Islaam, and this itself is speaking against the Messenger and talking badly about him, or it is being asserted that he was actually aware of this new belief or practice but chose not to convey to the people! This is also considered speaking against him and maligning him, because the one who believes this in fact claims that the Prophet did not convey to the humanity some part of Islaam that was revealed to him.

From the corrupting effects of innovation in the religion, is that it undoubtedly requires negating the statement of Allaah, the Most High, where he stated, ❴*...This day, I have perfected your religion for you, completed My Favor upon you, and have chosen for you Islaam as your religion.*❵-(Surah Al-Ma'idah: 3) The belief of one who is innovating a new belief or practice into Islaam necessitates the perspective that: the religion of Islaam is not truly complete since we did not find this innovation in the religion of Allaah previously. Therefore, if it is truly part of the religion of Allaah as claimed by the innovator, but it is not found in the sources of the religion, then the religion as they understand cannot be something which is complete and perfect. This is a major significant contradiction to the statement of Allaah, the Most High ❴*...This day, I have perfected your religion for you,...*❵-(Surah Al-Ma'idah: 3)

From the corrupting effects of innovation in the religion: is that the one who innovates in the religion places himself in a similar position as a messenger who was actually sent by Allaah, as it is not possible for anyone to legislate to the creation what will truly bring them closer to Allaah, the Most High, except the one who Allaah, the Most Glorified and the Most Exalted, Himself has sent with that revealed guidance. Yet there are no prophets sent with such guidance after Muhammad, may Allaah's praise and salutation be upon him and his family.

For this reason the one who innovates in the religion it is as if he is saying that he is bringing something legislated to the people which will bring them closer to Allaah, and this specifically asserts that he is someone who shares with the Messenger of Allaah, may Allaah's praise and salutations be upon him, the actual role of conveying Allaah's guidance, which they did not know before, to humanity!

From the corrupting effects of innovation in the religion, is the speaking about Allaah without true knowledge. Doing so is completely forbidden by the total consensus of all the Muslims throughout the ages. Allaah says the Blessed and the Most High, says, ❴ *Say (Oh Muhammad): "But the things that my Lord has indeed forbidden are great evil sins, every kind of unlawful sexual intercourse, whether committed openly or secretly, sins of all kinds, unrighteous oppression, joining partners in worship with Allaah for which He has given no authority, and saying things about Allaah of which you have no knowledge.* ❵ - (Surah Al-A'raf:33)

And there are certainly other corrupting effects of innovating in the religion which if someone was to closely examine them he would find that they add to these mentioned harmful effects significantly, but we have held ourselves to what has been mentioned here."

(4)

NINETY-NINE CHARACTERISTICS OF VARIOUS MISGUIDED GROUPS

The following complete appendix is taken from an appendix to the small work "*The Methodology of the People of the Sunnah and Adherence to the Jama'ah in Calling to Allaah.*" by 'Abdullah Ibn Muhammad Ibn Saaleh al-Ma'taar[1] with an introduction by the esteemed guiding scholar Sheikh Saaleh Ibn Fauzaan al-Fauzaan, may Allaah preserve him.

As is well-known, a matter is not understood except by comprehending that which opposes it. And in light of the fact of what we have presented of some of the characteristics of those who follow the first three generations of Muslims, the Salafees, then it is of some importance that we indicate some of the characteristics of those who oppose them in order to warn against these characteristics. Just as the well-known saying: through their opposites, matters become clear and understood.

Certainly Hudhaifah ibn al-Yamaan, may Allaah be pleased with him, would ask the Messenger of Allaah, made a praise and salutations of Allaah be upon him, about evil situations fearing that he would fall into them. For this reason we present in what follows some of the characteristics of the misguided groups upon which they have developed a methodology of calling and inviting to the religion which opposes the methodology of those who follow the first three generations. Generally they had neglected establishing the correct Islamic beliefs and calling to them and basing one's allegiance to others upon those beliefs. While at the same time these groups and movements have concentrated on issues of ruling and political power, or current societal affairs and situations.

---

[1] Published by Dar Ibn Jawzee, Cairo 1425

In doing so they have become significant agents working for the spread of innovations and aligning themselves with the people of innovation and placing them in positions of leadership. It has become one of their important priorities to gather and join together of significant numbers of people including within those whom they have assembled people who differ significantly, from people of various Sufeeyah paths, people of the sect of the Raafidhah, and those who worship at graves all together.

So it is clear that among them are those who have become those who love for other than the sake of Allaah, and become those who direct that love towards others despite that they are not the people truly worshiping Allaah alone. From within these groups and movements there are those who attack the scholars who adhere to the way of the Salaf, accusing them of being those who only curry favor from the rulers, and accusing the scholars of being those who only have a ritualistic or simplistic understanding of the religion.

They claim these scholars have been deceived regarding the affair of the Muslim rulers, and they accuse them of having a lack of understanding of the current situation of the Muslims, and a failure to properly grasp the overall situations regarding nations and countries. They claim that the scholars are ignorant of the plans of the enemies of Islaam and the secularists. For this reason they do not refer to them or take any important rulings related to the Muslim nation from them but only refer to them for rulings regarding matters such as ritual purification, women's menses, by claiming that these Salafee scholars do not understand the larger affairs which are going on around them. And we seek refuge in Allaah from this tremendous slander and false accusation.

At the same they themselves instigate and provoke the governments against those who call to the way of the Salaf, the first three generations, and chose to engage in economic strikes and political demonstrations, making unlawful actions permissible under the claim of seeking an overall better condition for the Muslims. Yet they chose to remain silent about those wrongdoings found within their own parties and groups as well as those errors found in the statements of their leaders, while accusing the people who call to the worship of Allaah alone as a priority, of being severe and harsh. From those within these groups, parties, and movements are those who criticize the early books of knowledge by labeling them as "weak" and "feeble". Yet they themselves are those who worship their intellects, their invented concepts, and their personal desires.

What follows are summarized characteristics related to one of more of these modern day groups, parties, and movements that call themselves "Islamic":

1. Among these groups are those who alter and change the meaning of the statement "*La ilaah illa Allaah*" from meaning the general comprehensive subservience to Allaah, the Most High, and the required negation and turning away from everything which is worshiped other than Him, to: simply meaning affirming his Lordship as the Creator and Sustainer. Thus they disregard and neglect both "*Tawheed al-Uluheeyah*" or the affirmation that Allaah alone is to be worshiped and obeyed, and "*Tawheed al-Asma'a wa Sifaat*" or the affirmation of understanding Allaah's names and attributes just as Allaah and His Messenger conveyed and explained them.

2. Among these groups are those who give significant importance to the societal and cultural affairs and situations in the Muslim countries, or what they have named "*Fiqh al-Waaqi'a*" "or the "understanding current affairs". They go to extremes and exaggerate the importance of this while lacking insight, not placing it in its appropriate restricted position and status. In their contrived comprehension of this "essential knowledge" they have become arrogant towards the established scholars who stand upon the Sunnah, despite the fact that they themselves are the most ignorant people in relation to comprehensive understanding of the sciences and knowledge of the Sharee'ah, true complete knowledge of the current situation of the Muslims, and current Islamic thought and discourse. They themselves do not give importance to cultivating the correct fundamental beliefs, nor gaining knowledge, nor utilizing specific evidences directly taken from the Book of Allaah, the Sunnah of the Messenger of Allaah, may the praise and salutations of Allaah be upon him, and the established Consensus of the Muslims. They wrongly explain having knowledge of current affairs as merely being aware of news and information related to societal and governmental issues, but fail to properly place and view this information in light of the guidance and evidences of the Sharee'ah.

3. Among these groups are those who occupy themselves within efforts to gain political power, and so expose themselves to harm and injuries without being truly concerned with guiding the people to that sound way to the true methodology of correct beliefs and behavior and seeking understanding of the evidences regarding matters in Islaam.

4. Among these groups are those who claim that their priority is rectifying the corrupt Muslim rulers, and speaking about their errors and transgressions, despite the fact that they do not place the same importance upon rectifying the people who are ruled in those same Muslim lands and cultivating them upon Islaam. They are also those whose misguided position towards the Muslim rulers present today is that they are all disbelievers without any exception, failing to distinguish in a detailed manner between this nation and that nation. They see no difference between the land of Saudi Arabia and other nations but hold in their view that all of these governments are only agents of the West and those who secretly conspire against Islaam. Any government who puts forth any action or endeavor which includes something of giving victory to Islaam then they claim this is only an act of hypocrisy and part of the plotting against the Muslims. The reason for this perspective is because they are students of and had been raised upon works of speculative thought and ideas of "Islamic " thinkers.

Their basic position is that of having an evil suspicion of all the rulers generally while refusing to consider the outward actions of the rulers as valid despite this being the methodology of the people of the Sunnah. And some of them hold that the only acceptable way is to overthrow the rulers, not to work towards their rectification. This is because as a false fundamental premise they do not believe in the validity of the oath of allegiance given to the Muslim ruler. For they wrongly believe that implementing any man-made laws, even partially to any degree, within a Muslim nation is major disbelief which takes you outside of Islam. This is simply because they have turned away from the established guidelines of the scholars regarding establishing what is disbelief in Islaam.

Similarly they wrongly view that any cooperation with the disbelievers, even in those matters which do not consist of disbelief as held by the people of the Sunnah, is still major disbelief which takes one outside of Islaam. They also hold that revolting against the unjust ruler is permissible even when it is not clearly established that he has committed open clear disbelief- if there is, as they claim, a possible benefit for the Muslims in doing so. As such they have reached a level of severe extremism in this issue. And we ask Allaah for health and well-being.

5. Among these groups are those who preoccupy themselves by requesting solely from the governments in Muslim lands that they implement the Islamic system and Sharee'ah without also seeking that from the members of that society who are individually distant from many aspects of Islaam in belief and practice. This call has instigated the rulers against some of the callers to Islaam and been the cause of their harassment, imprisonment, and even killing. Rather what they should have done is given priority and importance to the cultivation and education of the individuals and the guidance of society in general before anything else along with the giving advice to the rulers with wisdom and sound admonitions.

6. Among these groups are those who openly swear and take an oath within the assemblies of Parliament to protect and preserve the full constitution which they themselves believe has that within it which opposes the Sharee'ah of Allaah while refusing to openly indicate and clarify those matters which oppose the guidance of Islaam.

7. Among these groups are those who sit and cooperate in those governmental bodies which legislate matters for the people according to other than that which Allaah revealed without openly disapproving or speaking out against that opposition.

8. Among these groups are those whose actions have been the cause for many of the sincere Muslims to be thrown into prison and expelled from their homes, due to what those individuals undertook which lacked both insight and wisdom. Certainly there were no beneficial results for the Muslims from what they involved themselves in, only tremendous hardship and difficulty.

9. Among these groups are those who take a very lax and weak position towards innovation in the religion, superstitious practices, and acts of associating others with Allaah due to the claimed need to unite the voices and gather the Muslims in a single rank, or due to some other false pretext and claim. This occurs to such a degree that they have reached the state where they will even intentionally choose someone as their general leader from those people who engages in superstitious practices or performs sinful acts of associating others with Allaah.

10. Among these groups are those who implement the rule or false principle **"We cooperate with each other in that which we agree upon and we excuse each other regarding those matters in which we differ."** Rather what is obligatory in regards to the one who differs with a matter from the Sharee'ah, is that he is advised and then afterwards if he does not accept the evidenced truth then he is boycotted and enmity is shown towards him once the proof is established against him in his clear opposition to any fundamental or principle from the fundamentals and principles of Islaam.

11. Those who align themselves with those rulers who the scholars have established are indeed disbelievers and choose to aid and support them.

12. Among these groups are those who do not attach any importance to the presence of practices of associating others with Allaah, tombs which are revered, dangerous innovations, and graves which are worshiped within their lands. They focus on issues of lesser importance, while their lands drown in such innovated ways of worship, and in false acts of associating others with Allaah through supplicating to the dead, and other misguided acts.

13. Among these groups are those who do not give needed priority in what they write within their books or magazines, nor what they focus upon in conferences they hold, to taking the offensive in combating innovations in the religion and innovators, as well as opposing practices of associating others with Allaah and worship and those who engage in them. Among the individuals in these groups and movements, there is not seen those who establish any foundations for organizations with the essential priority of establishing sound beliefs among the people, meaning the beliefs of the people of the Sunnah and adherence to the Jama'ah. Likewise, within the schools they control and manage, they do not teach from the books of the first generations which establish the correct authentic belief.

14. Among these groups are those who engage in wasting money, excessive talking, exaggeration in speech and what is put out to the media advocating only their methodology and their calling to Allaah. They give greater importance to their outward image than informing people of the truth, and more emphasis on propaganda rather than actual beneficial endeavors. Similarly their general focus is more on conferences, awards, and fundraising drives, and outward demonstrations, than on actually establishing schools, opening masjids, and assisting those who call to the truth.

15. Among these groups are those who form nationalistic political alliances of cooperation with those who disbelievers in their own countries, and yet they do not rebuke and censure each other for making pacts with those with no connection to Islaam.

16. Among these groups are those who falsely suppose that they have the ability to unite the Muslim people together in some way other than the only true way which is establishing Muslim unity upon the pure correct beliefs of Islaam, and their actions and efforts reflect and stand in accord with this misconception.

17. Among these groups are those who attack the people engaged in political efforts in their lands but do not likewise attack the innovating Sufee groups, nor the people who worship at graves and engage in impermissible superstitious practices. This negligence enables innovations to increase in their lands and firmly take root among the people.

18. Among these groups are those who give little importance to the study of hadeeth sciences and its transmitted knowledge, while focusing upon various intellectual concepts, developed individual views, and philosophical perspectives.

19. Among these groups are those who excessively praise those individuals who are connected to their groups and parties and have extreme support of them, while at the same time defaming and speaking against anyone who criticizes these same leaders and party figureheads. They refuse to recognize their right and position as scholars, that they have due to their acknowledged knowledge and piety. This is especially true if the scholar who criticized one of them is a scholar from those who adhere to the methodology of the Salaf.

20. Among these groups are those who wrongly support the leaders of their groups, organizations, or parties who are known to have beliefs which are clearly deviated from the correct beliefs . Meaning individuals such as those who hold the beliefs of the Ashaarees, the Matureedees, the beliefs of innovators generally, or those who associate others with Allaah in acts of worship and consider it permissible to supplicate to the dead and seek intercession through them.

21. Among these groups are those who discuss the deceptive plots of Shaytaan and warn against them, yet also make the plots and plans of the Eastern and Western nations against the Muslims as something greater than the general deceptive plots of Shaytaan, the accursed the envious.

22. Among these groups are those who incite the impressionable common Muslims by advocating the path of demonstrations, protests, political activities, and other worthless and ineffective "revolutionary" methods that only cause trials. They delude and misguide them without bringing them any result other than individuals being thrown in prison, the people of goodness rounded up together, insulted and treated badly, and the governments oppressing them and others needlessly.

23. Among these groups are those who concentrate within their Friday sermons upon imagined inflammatory issues which incite people, without basing their statements upon sound evidences from the Sharee'ah as found within the Book of Allaah and the authentic Sunnah.

24. Among these groups are those whose methodology is to proceed upon the way of forming party and group based alliances and politically based confederations. They wrongly accept the method of sitting in consultative assemblies with those who are known enemies of the call to purify misconceptions in the Muslims fundamental beliefs and opponents of those focusing on calling Muslims to worship of Allaah alone without partners.

25. Among these groups are those who attack and assault the well known scholars of Islaam and work to defame the leading people of knowledge from amongst the Muslims. They seek to harm the followers of the way of the Salaf, those who adhere to hadeeth narrations, those who give importance to the correct beliefs and to explaining the religion upon evidences.

26. Among these groups are individuals who have a stronger allegiance to the leaders of their groups and organizations than their allegiance to the Messenger of Allaah, may the praise and salutations of Allaah be upon him, and towards the notable scholars of the esteemed first generations.

27. Among these groups are those who innovate matters in their efforts of calling to Allaah, standing upon a methodology which was not known in the time of the Messenger, may the praise and salutations of Allaah be upon him, nor was it known during the time of the rightly guided Khaleefahs who succeeded him.

28. Among these groups are those who wrongly make certain prohibited practices acceptable and permissible either in the name of achieving the greater good or by claiming necessity or by claiming that it is a matter which is subject to independent scholastic reasoning and assessment. Yet in reality these practices do not actually enter into any of these legitimate Sharee'ah causes or justifications.

29. Among these groups are those who refuse to censure and refute the mistakes of those within their organizations and groups even when these mistakes reach the level of opposing the authentic narrations of the Messenger of Allaah, may the praise and salutations of Allaah be upon him, or conflicting with the statements of the people of knowledge from the first three generations.

30. Among these groups are those who always seek and vigorously search for some excuse for a error for those individuals within their organizations and groups even if their mistake is a significant and considerable one which it is not possible to excuse. But when someone from outside of their organization or group makes the same mistake , they contradictorily strive to raise the entire world and its important people up against him because of it.

31. Among these groups are those who speak and engage themselves with the statements of the leaders of their organizations and groups more than they concern themselves and engage themselves with the statements of the Messenger of Allaah, may praise and salutations of Allaah be upon him, or the statements of the companions of the Messenger, may Allaah be pleased with them all, and the statements of those scholars of this Ummah who adhere to the way of the first generations of believers.

32. Among these groups are those who falsely accuse the people who adhere to the Sunnah with extremism, fanatical adherence, radicalism, and fanaticism, while at the same time they are those who have fallen into haphazardly declaring the Muslims disbelievers and go to actual extremes in matters, yet they do not criticize or blame themselves.

33. Among these groups are those who falsely claim that the established practice of implementing fiqh principles and the statements of the various scholars throughout the ages in these different matters are unnecessarily rigid pronouncements which do not properly take the changing circumstances of the ages and time into consideration. They describe them as books that are weak and shallow, or as books that mostly discuss issues of women's menses and bleeding, or as superficial works not based on valid understanding of the current situations of the Muslims.

34. Among these groups are those who only submit themselves to the guidance of the Sharee'ah in the various matters of religion when what it calls for or stands in agreement with their personal desires, their intellectual assessments, and their logical pronouncements.

35. Among these groups are those who incorrectly call the people to take any possible allowance in Sharee'ah matters rather than being resolutely patient and steadfast with a necessary hardship.

36. Among these groups are those who falsely lead the people to believe that the Salafees are incapable of comprehending the different modern societal conditions, and the new evolving situations and circumstances of our modern age.

37. Among these groups are those who invite the people to study Western ideas and foreign philosophies beneath the claim that the people can benefit from this. However at the same time they nearly abandon the statements of the Messenger of Allaah, may the praise and salutations of Allaah be upon him, and the statements of the scholars from the first three righteous generations. From the causes of this is the presence of the large number of those known as callers amongst the Muslims who possess very little knowledge of the transmitted narrations of the Prophet, and the transmitted statements from the early scholars. Yet these same individuals have become proficient and experts regarding the statements of the Westerners and whatever is related to modern politics which are based upon intellectual foundations coming from Jewish scholars as well as those affiliated with the Masons. And they focus on that Western knowledge by claiming to do so because of the need to understand the current affairs.

38. Among these groups are those who generally legitimize impermissible acts such as lying, spying, and other transgressions allegedly for the overall benefit of efforts to call to Allaah. In fact the often employ invented accusations and disgraced fabrications against those oppose their methodology.

39. Among these groups are those who encourage the efforts of the Shee'ah, support the Shee'ah ideology and the ideals of the Iranian revolution, and advocate revolution whenever possible against the rulers in Muslim lands at any time they believe this was feasible. Similarly, there are those among these groups who promote those efforts to increase the conceptual closeness between the understanding of Islaam held by the Sunnees and the Shee'ah, as well as interfaith conceptual closeness between the Muslims, Jews, and Christians.

40. Among these groups are those who do not stand clearly upon any firm evidenced position. They are easily deceived by the deceptions of the enemies of Allaah and their fabrications and so they fall into accepting them. Yet they do recant from and abandon these positions when the definitive proof is established to them by other Muslims. So they end up changing their "colors" or positions according to the situation and time. This is because their initial understandings were not based upon correct sound knowledge and Sharee'ah evidences or an unbiased objective perspective established for Allaah's sake alone.

Due to this you will see that in one instance or time they show enmity towards the sect of the Shee'ah, yet inconsistently they contradict this position at another time. For this reason, that they are not based upon correct sound knowledge and Sharee'ah evidences, you see that many of their strongly taken positions do not agree with that which is correct according to Sharee'ah evidences.

41. Among these groups are those who restrict themselves to only enjoining what is good while intentionally neglecting to forbid what is evil or wrongdoing while claiming that the forbidding of wrongdoing will cause separation and division, driving away the people who follow them.

42. Among these groups are those who establish their calls upon only specific matters or issues while neglecting other legitimate matters that may be more important and more significant in Islaam than those issues which they have focused upon and adopted.

43. Among these groups are those who chose to rely upon books which undoubtedly include within them false superstitions, innovations in the religion, and matters related to practices of associating others with Allaah in worship.

44. Among these groups are that affirm the practice of the Sufees to give the oath of allegiance to the head of their Sufee order or group as is found among the four major Sufee groups, The Naqshabandeeyah, the Qaadereeyah, the Saharoodeeyah, and the Chisteeyah - as well as among others from the Sufees.

45. Among these groups are those who view the danger of Sufism and general innovations in the religion as being less than the danger of other sins and transgressions.

46. Among these groups are those who believe that the acts of shirk related to personal possessions and belongings are more significant than that shirk related to matters of exaggeration towards the individuals considered close associates of Allaah and turning to the righteous people who have died for assistance.

47. Among these groups are those who invite to the way of acknowledging false miracles performed by the people of Sufeeyah, innovated methods of reaching different levels of spiritual consciousness and spiritual realizations, as well as affirming their claims of possessing knowledge of some of the hidden matters.

48. Among these groups are those individuals who offer weak efforts for those issues which are essential to the methodology of the Salafees, while strongly supporting and giving significant attention to all those matters focused upon by those not following the way of the Salafees. The result of this is that you see them at that time when they discuss those issues essential to the Muslims who follow the way of the Salaf, they unenthusiastically tell the people to proceed slowly and carefully. Yet at other times when they discuss positions of their specific party or group then for this they vigorously put forth moving sermons and eloquent poetry which incites the people with false enthusiasm and deceptions.

49. Among these groups are those who proceed upon a blind biased adherence to the specific historical school of jurisprudence. In the rulings they accept, they fail to give proper consideration of the actual evidences found within the Book of Allaah and the Sunnah. Similarly regarding the fundaments of the religion then they do not accept and take on any position except when they find it agrees with the desires and dictates of their specific scholars.

50. Among these groups are those who are callers to the religion and enjoin matters upon the people without insight and correct knowledge. They do not consider anyone from the scholars to truly be callers to the religion except for those whom their group judges as truly pious and devout.

51. Among these groups are those who in their writings and statements use fabricated hadeeth narrations and unverified superstitious stories, some who rely upon dreams, individual spiritual insights , and the statements of various scholars of Sufeeyah for determining the Sharee'ah validity of actions and rulings, rather than authentic transmitted knowledge.

52. Among these groups are those who do not censure nor speak against the presence of graves in their various well-known centers of religious activities and masjids.

53. Among these groups are those who distribute garments of hijaab that have talismans and mystical numbers sown upon them which they claim has protective power by connection to the old senile sheikhs of their misguided way.

54. Among these groups are those who rely upon the common people and ignorant to give their call and movement support. They neglect the priority of correct beliefs in terms of knowledge as well of their actions and efforts. So they lack any true power or authority over anyone except for some of the common people and people like this.

55. Among these groups are those who wrongly say regarding the respect shown to well known scholars: Certainly some of the people of knowledge have been given such high position, in terms of the people visiting them and going to them, which has not even been given to the sacred Kaa'ba!

56. Among these groups are those who call the people to generally blind follow others in their religion and do not call them to adhere to the evidences found in the source texts of the Qur'aan and Sunnah.

57. Among these groups are those who innovated a new method and way of sending salutations upon the Messenger of Allaah, may Allaah praise and salutations be upon him that is not legislated. Such is found in their saying : "Oh Allaah send Your praise upon our Sayideena (leader) Muhammad from Your oceans of light, from the mines of Your secret mysteries, from the tongues of Your evidences and demonstrations, from the throne of Your Majesty, from in front of Your presence, from that exquisiteness of Your dominion, from the treasures of Your mercy, from the path of Your Sharee'ah, the one made zestful and zealous by Your Oneness, the man who was the heart of existence, the reason for all existence, the master of the notable ones from Your creation, the one who proceeded forth from the

light of Your illumination. Oh messenger of Allaah we ask you for your intercession."

This is found in the book 'Tableeghee Nisaaab', in the section of the merits of Hajj. And on another page in the same work there is found the following two blameworthy lines of poetry about the Prophet:

And when we saw in the return of our beloved one
his exquisite goodness raised within us such love by his closeness to us
that our restless eyes relished our intercession through him
such that there is no torment or punishment that we fear

58. Among these groups are those who falsely view some forbidden acts of seeking for wealth and material prosperity through other than Allaah to be equal to those false acts of association of others with Allaah directed to false idols.

59. Among these groups are those who wrongly equate the verses of the Qur'aan that mention going forth physically in Jihaad the way of Allaah with going out for efforts of da'wah and sleeping overnight in the masjids.

60. Among these groups are those who believe in the legitimacy of going to grave sites for the purpose of asking and supplication.

61. Among these groups are those who have wrongly taken an individual who spoke with the concept of the unity of creation with the creator- as a spiritual and ideological leader and guide for them.

62. Among these groups are those who wrongly restrict the meaning of the Shahaadah the testimony of faith in Islaam, saying "*La ilaha ill Allaah*": to mean only one of the following three things:
1. That what is intended or important by this is that one has certain belief that there is no Creator and Sustainer of the physical universe other than Allaah.
2. That what is important is that the one who makes this statement before his death will enter into Jannah simply due to its merit.
3. In terms of a phrase that you can achieve something by through physically pronouncing it: meaning its repetition in an innovated act of ritual remembrance or dhikr of this noble Shahaadah or a shorted form of it by saying, "*Allaah Allaah Allaah*" or "*Huwa Huwa Huwa*" or a similar variation.

63. Among these groups are those who believe that journeying for Allaah's sake does not require anything other than being present in the Masjid, leaning on one of its pillars with your head bowed in ritual dhikr. They see this as the main activity of value of their "journey" and what gives it its true value.

64. Among these groups are those who request that the followers of their Sufee way read Surah Yaseen at night every Thursday, despite that fact that this is an innovation in the religion and that no one, starting with the Companions of the Prophet, from the first three generations ever did it.

65. Those who request that the followers of their Sufee way take a trip to the graveyard once every week, and while there they repeat the phrase: "Allaah is present , Allaah is the beholder", as is known to be done from some of the leaders and their individual followers among those who connect themselves to some of the misguided groups.

66. Among these groups are those who knowingly pray in masjids which are built upon grave sites, and how many there are of these among the Muslims! And some of these people have lessons in these masjids, and then participate in the distribution of pieces of the material from those gravesites which are present in these masjids as blessings, without them criticizing or rejecting this in any way.

67. Among these groups are those who seek the living intercession of the Messenger of Allaah, may the praise and salutations of Allaah be upon him, in this era even though he has died. As indeed Allaah has said, "Say, to Allaah belongs all intercession." –(Surah az-Zumaar: 44(and the remaining intercession is on the Day of Judgement.

68. Among these groups are those who prefer to seek help by supplication to the Messenger of Allaah, may the praise and salutations of Allaah be upon him, rather than supplicating directly to Allaah. And this act is considered a major sin of associating others in worship with Allaah that many who consider themselves Muslim fall into. Yet it is not only many who consider themselves Muslim, who fall into this misguidance, but many who are considered "leaders" of Islamic groups, movements, and organizations!

69. Among these groups are those who believe in the superstitious claims of Ahmad ar-Rafaa'aee the deluded one who claimed that the Messenger of Allaah, may the praise and salutations of Allaah be upon him, pushed his hand out from his grave so that Ahmad ar-Rafaa'aee could kiss it!!

70. Among these groups are those individuals who regularly go to the places of the Sheikhs in order to request "signs" of direction from them for what choices to make in the smallest aspects of their lives, such as marriage or divorce, continuing one's studies or stopping, seeking such and such employment or leaving it. These people enthusiastically visit and travel to them and kiss their hands, due to the belief among them that these "Sheikhs" have knowledge of the hidden affairs and can benefit the people in their affairs.

71. Among these groups are those who give strong consideration to individuals from the people of innovation in the religion, and they follow the directives of these people against the efforts of the people of Tawheed.

72. Among these groups are those who actually fight against the people who oppose the people's acts of associating others with Allaah, falsely attempting to use as their proof for this position the statement of Allaah, the Most High, "And insult not those whom they (disbelievers) worship besides Allaah, lest they insult Allaah wrongfully without knowledge…"-(Surah al-Ana'am: 108)

73. Among these groups are those who spend the entire night until morning reciting Qur'aan in a single sitting specifically due to the death of one of the sheikhs of their group or movement.

74. Those who warn the people against authentic transmitted knowledge and the scholars of that knowledge, as they label Sharee'ah-based knowledge as "the knowledge of outward issues" while referring to knowledge of the beliefs and practices of Sufism as "the knowledge of true realities".

75. Among these groups are those who search within the texts of the Book of Allaah and the Sunnah to find that which agrees with their desires and wishes and they attempt to forget or ignore whatever texts and evidences oppose them. They refuse to submit and comply with any authentic evidence if it differs with their positions or the views of their movement or organization and its leaders.

76. Among these groups are those who refuse to submit to the judgment of Allaah and His Messenger in those matters in which they differ with their Muslim brothers. Yet Allaah, the Most High, says, *But no, by your Lord, they can have no Faith, until they make you (Oh Muhammad) judge in all disputes between them, and find in themselves no resistance against your decisions, and accept them with full submission.*-(Surah an-Nisa': 65)

77. Among these groups are those who, in their efforts of calling to Allaah, place great emphasis on the issue of "*Tawheed ar-Rububeeyah*" or acknowledging that Allaah is the Lord of all the worlds. They speak frequently about how tremendous and powerful a Creator and Lord He is, without indicating the need to submit to Him through worshiping Him alone.

But they do not frequently speak about "*Tawheed al-Uuheeyah*" or affirming and acknowledging that Allaah alone must be worshiped without any partners, nor about "*Tawheed Asmaa wa Sifaat*", or believing in Allaah's names and attributes fully without misinterpretation just as they have been conveyed and explained by Allaah Himself and His Messenger.

78. Among these groups are those that say: These Salafees who are focusing on calling first to the worship of Allaah alone cause separation between the Muslims of different groups and movements. Or they claim that the Salafees have an overly strict adherence to the guidelines of Islaam. And if a single individual from among the Salafees makes a mistake, they aggrandize it trying to make it a significant issue and then attempt to connect or attach his incorrect action or behavior to the call of adhering to the way of the Salaf itself.

79. Among these groups are those who make it a priority simply to gather Muslim people superficially together, and then connect them to a party or group through calling for them to give an oath of allegiance to its leader, without actually establishing their unity upon acceptance and submission to the firm principles and foundations of Islaam!

80. Among these groups are those who base their allegiance and disassociation with other Muslims, as something foremost based upon the Muslim's relationship to their organization, their group, or their movement rather than the practice loving and hating any and all individuals for the sake of Allaah and His religion only, and then interacting with the people on that basis.

81. Among these groups are those specific individuals who have chosen to name themselves and their group "*Jama'at al-Muslimeen*". Yet when their specific beliefs and practices are examined, it is seen that they have differed with the Muslims from the people of the Sunnah in matters with clear fundamentals, and in authentic affirmed beliefs.

82. Among these groups are those who falsely label the Salafees, meaning the people of hadeeth- those who call to adherence to the evidence found within the Book of Allaah and the Sunnah and to reject and turn away from anything which differs with the guidance of these two sources- they label them as "*those without any madhhaab*", or "*Wahaabees*", "*those with hatred towards the Prophet's family*", in order to scare and drive the people away from them.

83. Among these groups are those who do not pay attention to any issues of knowledge except when it comes directly from the people of their organization or group. And they actually blame and speak against those who bring forth those issues of knowledge whenever it comes from other than themselves.

84. Among these groups are those who ally themselves politically and become confederates with the enemies of Allaah in a country to stand against other Muslims during the process of national or parliamentary elections as well as the other times, This is due to their fear of the emergence and growing prominence in the land of any Muslims other than the members from their specific group or party.

85. Among these groups are those who work to defame and tarnish the reputations of those individuals striving to spread the correct Salafee methodology amongst the Muslims.

86. Among these groups are those who believe in the false principle that "the ends justify the means."

87. Among these groups are those who show enmity and scheme against anyone who does not work with their organization or group. They defame and slander everyone who opposes them and they falsely legitimize attacking both their honor and reputation.

88. Among these groups are those who give importance to their outward appearance among the people without truly considering actual beneficial results as judged by Islaam, and give importance to having conferences without focusing on the people implementing the advices of the scholars.

89. Among these groups are those who claim to follow the Qur'aan only. These are the individuals who separate between the Qur'aan and the Sunnah, saying we accept and work with that which is found in the Qur'aan but not that which is found in the Sunnah.

90. Among these groups are those who accept the use of authentic singularly transmitted narrations in the area of religious rulings in, but reject accepting those same authentic narrations in the area of beliefs, falsely restricting that to that class of authentic narrations with a high number of routes of transmission.

91. Among these groups are those who deny those future matters clearly affirmed in the Book and the Sunnah such as the attributes of Allaah, matters of the unseen, the punishment of Hellfire, the lesser and greater signs of the Day of judgment: such as the decent of 'Isaa, the Beast of the earth, and the Sun rising from the direction of the west. Similarly those individuals who deny those hadeeth narrations which are transmitted authentically about Allaah which are understood in a manner that befits His majesty and transcendence, such as the authentic narrations describing Allaah's descending in the last third of the night, or that He stretches out His Hand in the night, or that the hearts of the worshippers are between His two fingers, that He laughs, and other authentic narrations which are affirmed and correct, but understood in a manner befitting Allaah's' transcendence above creation.

92. Among these groups are those that attribute infallibility to someone other than Messenger of Allaah, may the praise and salutations of Allaah be upon him, such as their close associates and supporters, and ideological guides, or leaders of their way, and in doing so they have made them partners receiving worship other than Allaah.

93. Among these groups are those who instigate and agitate the people against the rulers and the scholars, either through mocking them or speaking against them in general sermons. Also, there are those who attempt to pit one scholar and his statements against another scholar and his statements, dividing up the young to stand upon the foundations of separate and different parties and affiliations. These separations and divisions into groups is a matter whose misguidance is based in the historical period of ignorance before the coming of Islaam. They generally exaggerate the importance of political analysis, and what they have named knowledge of current affairs, and focus on matters that have many claims and outwards calls but few if any real results.

94. Among these groups are those who go beyond the proper bounds of the true Sharee'ah position with the Messenger of Allaah, and show extremism in relation to the Prophet, may the praise and salutations of Allaah be upon him. Yet on hand they transgress and exaggerate and make him a partner to Allaah, the Most High, while on the other hand they openly reject and turn away from authentic commandments coming from Prophet that are for every Muslim, and do not actually adhere closely to his guidance and his general way.

95. Among these groups are those who bring into the religion of Islam that which has not based in revealed guidance. They seek to become closer to Allaah as they claim, through these various acts of innovation and superstitious practices which Allaah has not sent down any authority for then doing.

96. Among these groups are those who wrongly turn away from permissible aspects of worldly life found in the Sunnah without a proper Sharee'ah reason, and they encourage the people to love the living of a life of excessive abjectness, unnecessary lowliness, and undue meekness.

97. Among these groups are those who wrongly refuse to use the permissible modern technical means in efforts of calling to Allaah.

98. Among these groups are those individuals who have been tricked and deceived into the misconception that the Salafees hate the Messenger of Allaah, may the praise and salutations of Allaah be upon him. This is despite the fact that the Salafees are those who adhere to and follow him truly and with a true and sincere love of him, and are the ones who follow his Sunnah and way, and the guidance sent to him and his revealed methodology.

The Salafees sacrifice themselves, their wealth, and their time for the sake of supporting the guidance given to the Prophet. They are the ones that hold that loving the Messenger of Allaah comes before loving oneself, one's family, one's wealth, and one's parents. They are the ones who hold that it is a condition for the correctness of one's ritual prayers that the one praying send salutations upon the Prophet may the praise and salutations of Allaah be upon him, and that he was the best of the creation, the noblest of creation, the purest of creation, and the one from creation who had the most fear of Allaah. May the praise and salutations of Allaah be upon him, his household, and all those who follow his guidance until the Day of Judgment.

99. Among these groups are those who gather huge sums of money from Muslims and give them to the people of innovation in the religion and those who are enemies of those Muslims who call to the way of the first three generations. They at times knowingly make it impermissible to give to our Muslim brothers from amongst the Salafees around the world. Or at times they give wealth to the people of innovation and deviance in the religion while at the same time giving wealth to the Salafees.

This is done with the excuse of seeking to unite the Muslims or another excuse from the false excuses which they use in those efforts they undertake. This only results in the strengthening of those who oppose the Muslims who proceed upon the path of the Salaf as-Saaleh, first three generations of Islaam.

(5)

IT IS NOT FROM THE WAY OF THE FIRST THREE GENERATIONS TO…"

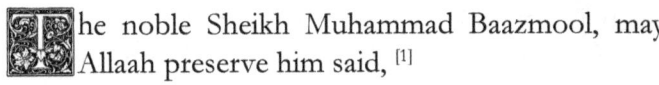

The noble Sheikh Muhammad Baazmool, may Allaah preserve him said, [1]

1. It is not from the way of the first three generations of Muslims to simply take knowledge from anyone and everyone until after you have looked at his condition and position in relation to the Sunnah. As it has been rightly said: "This knowledge is your religion, so look carefully as to whom you take knowledge of your religion."

2. It is not from the way of the first three generations of Muslims to neglect or fall short in speaking about the right of Allaah alone to be worshiped, and making this a firm reality in the souls of the people. As this matter, Tawheed, is the very foundation upon which each and every Muslims' Islaam is built upon.

3. It is not from the way of the first three generations of Muslims to engage in acting before having the necessary knowledge. Indeed, they were those who always began with knowledge before actions and deeds. As Allaah, the Most High, has said, ﴾ *(So know (O Muhammad) that none has the right to be worshipped but Allaah, and ask forgiveness for your sin, and also for the sin of believing men and believing women* ﴿-(Surah Muhammad: 19).

4. It is not from the way of the first three generations of Muslims to leave or turn away from patterning ourselves upon and closely following the Messenger of Allaah, may the praise and salutations of Allaah be upon him.

---

[1] The following points were all taken directly from the sheikhs' social media pages & website

5. It is not from the way of the first three generations of Muslims to speak against the Companions of the Messenger of Allaah, or even a single one of them.

6. It is not from the way of the first three generations of Muslims to invent and innovate new matters into the religion. From their distinguishing signs is that they followed transmitted knowledge. They did not innovate, finding fully sufficient what had been conveyed to them, so adhere truly to the original state of Islaam and the first believers.

7. It is not from the way of the first three generations of Muslims to give priority to intellectual sciences which are based primarily upon research and investigation; rather their foundations of knowledge were *"Allaah said..."* , *"The Messenger said..."*, & *"The Companion s said..."*

8. It is not from the way of the first three generations of Muslims to determine or identify the truth by men, such that everything that so-and-so brings must be the truth. Rather one of their distinguishing signs is that they held that a person who understands the truth will then be able to assess and determine those individuals in his time who hold and stand upon the truth , and that through understanding the truth you can become from the people who stand clearly upon it.

9. It is not from the way of the first three generations of Muslims to invent new guidelines and developed principles according to one's opinion. The way of the Salaf was to closely follow the established terminology found in the Qur'aan and Sunnah, such that in their rulings and statements they did not give meanings to verses or hadeeth narrations that were inconsistent and not possibly correct.

10. It is not from the way of the first three generations of Muslims to turn away and abandon adhering to the path of Islaam which the Companions proceeded upon, by conceiving a new understanding outside of what they understood in terms of comprehending the Sharee'ah.

11. It is not from the way of the first three generations of Muslims to derive a ruling or position from every single individual verse or hadeeth narration, until it is shown that is it a verse from the clear unambiguous verses or a hadeeth from those hadeeth narrations containing a definitive meaning which must be adhered to.

12. It is not from the way of the first three generations of Muslims to reject a hadeeth narration which doesn't make sense to our individual minds and intellects, or opposes and contradicts what we understand. Rather their methodology was to follow and affirm every authentic source text. We believe in every aspect of revealed guidance, as its origin is our Lord.

13. It is not from the way of the first three generations of Muslims to enter extensively into speculative discussions and opinion-based debates. Rather they put forth the utmost effort into fundamentally understanding Islaam from the Book of Allaah and the Sunnah, then acting according to these two sources and inviting the people to them.

14. It is not from the way of the first three generations of Muslims to go outside of and beyond what is indicated by the source texts as understood in the fundamentals of the Arabic language alongside the understanding that our righteous predecessors had of those source texts.

15. It is not from the way of the first three generations of Muslims to speak in generalizations and turn away from speaking specifically with detailed explanations.

16. It is not from the way of the first three generations of Muslims to neglect and turn away from actions, deeds, and implementation due to seeking knowledge. It is narrated that they said: *"Knowledge calls out for actions and deeds, such that actions come to stand with it. Otherwise without being accompanied by deeds- knowledge itself eventually leaves and departs."*

17. It is not from the way of the first three generations of Muslims to engage in a great deal of speech and talking. Indeed they used to say, *"The one who speaks frequently makes frequent mistakes and errors."* Some of them were known to remain silent to the degree that people would think that they were unintelligent or feebleminded. Yet this was not the case, their silence was only due to their fear of Allaah regarding the speech.

18. It is not from the way of the first three generations of Muslims too busy and occupy yourself with that which will not benefit you in the next life.

19. It is not from the way of the first three generations of Muslims that every student of knowledge enter into the arena of criticizing and commending individuals. Certainly in every area of Sharee'ah knowledge there are individuals well-known for their proficiency and understanding. So just as we do not generally take knowledge from any and every person, likewise in this area it is not for just anyone to speak in the matters of criticism and commendation of individuals.

20. It is not from the way of the first three generations of Muslims that the student of knowledge become preoccupied with secondary knowledge before focusing upon the study of the Qur'aan and hadeeth narrations. Once he has understood and learned that which is required for him in his religion, then he can seek that desired additional knowledge afterwards.

21. It is not from the way of the first three generations of Muslims to dispute with and oppose the scholars in their guiding statements. Indeed the student should know that he is indeed only a student and in regard to investigating and speaking about some issues, he should leave them to be dealt with by the scholars. It is not for him to enter into the current societal issues and problems among the Muslims nor discuss those significant wide-reaching matters!

22. It is not from the way of the first three generations of Muslims to form parties, secret alliances, and concealed gatherings and efforts separate from others. As it is found in the scholars of the first generations that they said, "*If you see a group of people who gather together in a masjid separating and excluding the general people, then know that they are upon misguidance.*"

23. It is not from the way of the first three generations of Muslims to incite and agitate the general Muslims against the ruler and instigate them to oppose him and revolt, or encourage them to engage in demonstrations and the bringing about of a revolution in society. Nor is it from their way to engage in public criticism of the rulers, their government ministers, or those who work for the governments under the rulers.

24. It is not from the way of the first three generations of Muslims to abandon seeking knowledge which is considered obligatory individually, nor that someone be neglectful of seeking knowledge which is generally recommended.

25. It is not from the way of the first three generations of Muslims to start attacking the scholars of the Sunnah and speak negatively about them, dismissing their knowledge and their books, calling for their books to be destroyed and burnt, and saying that the people should stop referring to them simply due to a restricted mistake or error that a known scholar fell into.

26. It is not from the way of the first three generations of Muslims to deal with the mistakes of the people of adherence to the Sunnah in the same way one deals with the mistakes of the people of innovation. As all the sons of Adam make mistakes, so look into the way and methodology of the mistaken individual and deal with that mistake which he has fallen into in a way suitable and in accordance to the general methodology he follows and adheres to.

27. It is not from the way of the first three generations of Muslims to have fanaticism and extremism to a specific derived view or position you hold, considering it above question. As we find those who spoke from the early people of knowledge would say: "*My position is correct with some possibility of it being wrong. And that position which opposes my position is wrong yet has some possibility of it being correct.*"

28. It is not from the way of the first three generations of Muslims to declare people as disbelievers in Islaam except upon what is explicitly considered disbelief in the Sharee'ah.

29. It is not from the way of the first three generations of Muslims make a judgment or declare a specific person as a disbeliever, and outside of the religion, except after having established the proofs against them by fulfilling the conditions and lifting any impediments required to make that declaration of disbelief.

30. It is not from the way of the first three generations of Muslims make a judgment or declare a specific person as an innovator in the religion except after having established the proofs against them by fulfilling the conditions and lifting any impediments required to make that declaration.

31. It is not from the way of the first three generations of Muslims fall into extremism regarding the status of the Messenger of the Allaah, may the praise and salutations of Allah be upon him, by placing him in a position or on a level equal with Allaah the Most High.

32. It is not from the way of the first three generations of Muslims to attribute or treat anyone as infallible other than the Messenger of Allaah, may the praise and salutations of Allaah be upon him.

33. It is not from the way of the first three generations of Muslims to make the focus of our call the redistribution of wealth even if done in the name of rectifying economic injustices. Nor is it from their way to make the focus of our call political engagement even if it is done in the name of rectifying wrongs by those governing the Muslims affairs.

34. It is not from the way of the first three generations of Muslims to develop a new practice of giving an oath of allegiance to someone other than that Muslim leader in society who is been entrusted with governing the Muslims and the affairs of their united group.

35. It is not from the way of the first three generations of Muslims to honor or hold in high esteem anyone who proceeds upon innovation in the religion of Islaam.

36. It is not from the way of the first three generations of Muslims to excuse someone due to ignorance unrestrictedly without any limitations or conditions. But we excuse, due to ignorance, the one who fell into error and missed what is right and correct after they put forth sufficient efforts in learning and seeking knowledge and didn't fall short in that. Such that the deficiency from such a person is clearly due to that inadequate knowledge which he received.

37. It is not from the way of the first three generations of Muslims to engage in debating with the people of falsehood. As the Muslims does not expose his sound religion to the danger of desires and doubtful matters.

38. It is not from the way of the first three generations of Muslims to turn away from referring to and returning to the scholars. Rather they were those who called the people to the sittings and lessons of the scholars, and for them to be in their gatherings.

39. It is not from the way of the first three generations of Muslims to act upon only the statement of praise which commends someone when there was also a detailed evidenced criticism against that individual. This is except in those cases when that detailed criticism has been brought to and mentioned to the scholar who originally commended and praised the individual, such that the commending scholar refuted that specific criticism with other specific knowledge and evidences.

40. It is not from the way of the first three generations of Muslims to act upon a general criticism of an individual whose trustworthiness has been affirmed, except when that general criticism is explained in detail, or was stated by a major or leading scholar which would lead you to be inclined to accept it due to confidence in the leading scholars' understanding and trustworthiness.

41. It is not from the way of the first three generations of Muslims to rely upon the people of innovation from the Muslims nor to unrestrictedly engage and deal with them.

42. It is not from the way of the first three generations of Muslims to turn away, in the matters of Muslim beliefs, from relying upon those authentic hadeeth narrations classified by the scholars of hadeeth as singular, in relation to their routes of transmission.

43. It is not from the way of the first three generations of Muslims to restrict what is considered as definitive knowledge from transmitted texts to only those authentic narrations classified by the scholars of the sciences of hadeeth as having multiple authentic routes of transmission, and reject authentic singular narrations.

44. It is not from the way of the first three generations of Muslims to reject what is transmitted from a reliable individual about someone and to not accept it, rejecting it unless it is heard or read personally by them from the original person.

45. It is not from the way of the first three generations of Muslims to love the people of innovation, nor to have a good opinion of them, nor to be misled by their shouts and cries, nor by their outward declarations. As they affirmed that a person would be with the one whom he loves, as is mentioned in the hadeeth narration.

46. It is not from the way of the first three generations of Muslims to act as if you are superior to the rest of the people. They were those who acted with goodness and gentleness.

47. It is not from the way of the first three generations of Muslims to seek fame and seek to elevate one's status among the people. As certainly love of fame "breaks ones back". So if you slip into this murky condition then it will certainly destroy tremendous amounts of good.

48. It is not from the way of the first three generations of Muslims to rely and focus upon the worldly life while abandoning those actions which benefit us in the Hereafter.

49. It is not from the way of the first three generations of Muslims to always engage in enmity simply because of the occurrence of a dispute that happened between them. Rather they would differentiate in having enmity with others according to the specific situation of the individual involved and the specifics and factors of the issue involved. As differing with the one with a pure intention for the truth upon its path does not ruin good relations in this case.

50. It is not from the way of the first three generations of Muslims to restrict the religion to a single minor issue which if someone agrees with me in that issue then he is considered Salafee and the one who differs with me in that issue then he is not considered Salafee. Rather Salafeeyah is a way and methodology and is not merely a single minor issue.

51. It is not from the way of the first three generations of Muslims to remain silent not offering advice and sincere counsel for the sake of Allaah, His Messenger, His Book, for the leaders of the Muslims and their common people.

52. It is not from the way of the first three generations of Muslims to fall into division, unnecessary differing and mutual hatred among themselves. From the distinguishing signs of the Salaf is that they never fell into hating each other and mutual hostility, rather they were worshipers of Allaah standing together as brothers.

53. It is not from the way of the first three generations of Muslims to involve themselves in trials and troubles, nor to enter and delve into them. Rather they were those who distanced themselves from trials and warned against entering into them.

54. It is not from the way of the first three generations of Muslims to choose blind following of others without following and turning to the evidences. Nor did they have biased attachments and allegiances.

(6)

THE REALITY OF SECULARISM: "WE WARN AGAINST THIS IDEOLOGICAL COLONIZATION…"

Sheikh 'Abdul-'Azeez Ibn Baaz, May Allaah Have Mercy Upon Him

Sheikh 'Abdul-'Azeez Ibn Baaz, may Allaah have mercy upon him, said:[1]

"Regarding the socialist Ba'ath Party, the ideology of Communism, as well as the other atheist ideologies which disbelieve in Islaam, such as secularism and others, it is established that all of them oppose Islaam and that those who adhere to these ideologies are in fact more severe in disbelief than the Christians and Jews. Since in relation to the Christians and Jews it is permissible for us to consume the animals they slaughter and eat their food generally and the Muslims are allowed to marry the chaste women from among them. But as for those who are atheists, is neither permissible to eat their food nor to marry their women. Similarly, this is the same case for those who are pagans worshipping aspects of nature, as a class of individuals, their women have not been made permissible to marry nor their food permissible to eat. As such every individual upon an atheistic ideology and so disbelieving in Islaam is considered more sinful, due to his disbelief, than a Christian or Jew.

These are those from the Ba'ath party and the secularists who reject Islaam and throw it behind their backs desiring something other than the religion of Islaam. This includes those who are known as communists, and socialists, meaning every atheistic ideological orientation which does not believe in Allaah, nor believe in the Day of Judgment. Their evil and disbelief is considered more significant and severe than the disbelief from the Jews and Christians.

---

[1] Collection of the Rulings of Sheikh Ibn Baaz: volume 6, page 85

Similarly, it should be noted that those who worship aspects of nature as pagans, those who worship and venerate graves and the dead within them, and those who worship and venerate trees or stones, they likewise are greater in disbelief than the Christians and Jews. It is for this reason that Allaah has established a distinction in the various distinct rulings of Islaam regarding interaction with them. Certainly, they all stand united upon their general disbelief and are misguided and the final destination for all of them is the Hellfire. Yet they are of different levels in their disbelief and degrees of their misguidance. However it is still the case, that they all stand upon clear disbelief and misguidance, and if they die in this state of misguidance, then their final destination is Hellfire."
\

Sheikh 'Abdul-'Azeez ar-Raajihee, May Allaah preserve Him

Sheikh 'Abdul-'Azeez ar-Raajihee, may Allaah preserve him, discussing the secularists, explained the following:: [2]

"These individuals, those with an outward profession of Islaam but who are inwardly upon disbelief, when they first appeared they were identified and called hypocrites "*munafiqoon*". Later historically as is found in the time period of Imaam Ahmad and afterwards an individual similar to this was referred to and called by a term which was originally a Farsi language term but later adopted by the Arabs "*Zindeeq*" meaning an astray disbeliever professing Islaam despite having significant innovation at the level of major disbelief.

---

[2] From his explanation of the work "The Belief of the First Three Generations and the People of Hadeeth" by as-Saaboonee as found in the fourteenth lecture

It has come to pass that in our time, some of those from this type are referred to and called "secularists". The secularists are clearly those who are hypocrites, and they are the "*Zanadeeqah*" or those who profess Islaam but inwardly are disbelievers. The hypocrites in the original time of the Prophet, may Allaah's praise and salutations be upon him, were individuals such as: Abdullah Ibn Ubay who outwardly manifested Islaam yet inwardly within themselves they still disbelieved. And the term "*zindeeq*" is generally applied to mean someone who is a disbelieving atheist.

Today those known as secularists have spread themselves among the Muslims. They attempt to insinuate themselves and place themselves with the Muslims and Islaam, in order to change and so corrupt the Muslims. They intend to alter the societal role of women and so corrupt the Muslim woman by sending her out of her home improperly dressed, habitually exposing her beauty to other women, needlessly driving vehicles and traveling, and unrestrictedly mixing with men outside her family. The result of these things they advocate will be the eventual corruption and degradation of society. Since if the Muslim woman is corrupted then undoubtedly the society itself is corrupted. The secularists have no actual ideological connection or inward adherence to the religion of Islaam, as they are "*zanaadeqah*". Yet they are not able to openly make fully evident what they truly upon of disbelief and hypocrisy, due to the strength of the Muslims. Because if they unmistakably made apparent their disbelief in the guidance of Islaam they fear that their necks would be struck and their lives lost as the believers and the people of goodness are numerous in Muslim societies. For this reason we find that they equivocate and minimize the reality of their disbelief, while they continually strive to corrupt and insinuate their evil among the Muslims through subtle means and refined methods."

Sheikh Saaleh Ibn al-Fauzaan, May Allaah preserve Him

Sheikh Saaleh Ibn al-Fauzaan was asked:[3]

Our esteemed sheikh, may Allaah grant you success, is it correct to generalize describing the secularist and the liberals, and even the individual extreme Shee'ah, with the term "hypocrite"?

He replied: "Such people in reality, do not reflect or outwardly show emaan, or faith. What they actually make apparent is their filthy ideologies and what they call for from abandoning Islaam, cursing and speaking against Islaam, as well as cursing the people firmly connected to the religion of Islaam. This is what such people reflect and make apparent. As such, they are not merely from the hypocrites, rather they are worse than them. They are from the "*zanaadeqah*" or astray disbelievers who despite professing Islaam, stand upon significant innovation which is at the level of major disbelief."

He also stated in one of his lectures,[4]

"Knowingly attributing yourself to one of the atheistic ideologies, such as communism, secularism, capitalism, or another disbelieving ideology, is apostasy from the religion of Islaam. If someone from those individuals who connect themselves to and believe in these other ideologies also stand forward as being someone who attributes himself to Islaam, then this is major hypocrisy. As the hypocrites are those known to attach themselves to Islaam outwardly, while internally and ideologically they stand with the disbelievers. Just as Allaah mentions regarding them: ***And when they meet those who believe, they say: "We believe," but when they are alone with their Shayaateen they say: "Truly,***

---

[3] From his published work "Aqeedatul-Tawheed, page 82
[4] Transcribed from the lecture "Selections from the Narrated Reports from the Leader of the Sent Messengers- Shawwal 1432

we are with you; verily, we were but mocking ❫-(Surah Al-Baqarah: 14) And Allaah the Most High said: ❮*Those hypocrites who wait and watch about you; if you gain a victory from Allaah, they say: "Were we not with you?" but if the disbelievers gain a success, they say to them: "Did we not gain mastery over you and did we not protect you from the believers?" Allaah will judge between you all on the Day of Resurrection. And never will Allaah grant to the disbelievers a way to triumph over the believers.* ❫-(Surah An-Nisa:141)

Such insincere individuals are deceptive hypocrites, each of them has two distinct faces: One face, which they show and direct towards the believers in Islaam, and another face which they turn to reveal with their associates upon their atheistic beliefs. They have two tongues, one, with superficial statements, which they use when speaking with the Muslims, and a second with which they make clear and expose what they hide of their concealed secret reality. As Allaah says, ❮*And when they meet those who believe, they say: "We believe," but when they are alone with their Shayaateen they say: "Truly, we are with you; verily, we were but mocking.*❫-(Surah Al-Baqarah:14)

Such individuals upon these ideologies have turned away and rejected the guidance of the Book of Allaah and the Sunnah, while they mock and belittle those who adhere to these fundamental sources of Islaam, holding such believing people in contempt. They are those who refuse to submit and fully comply with the guidance found in the two sources of revelation, the Qur'aan and the Sunnah. Rather they are more satisfied and actually pleased with whatever they possess of contrived worldly knowledge, despite it being something which their increasing themselves in it does not actually benefit them but only increases them in misguidance and arrogant rejection of the truth.

So we see that they look at those who firmly adhere to the revealed sources of guidance as those who should be mocked and ridiculed. Yet in truth- ❨*Allaah mocks at them and gives them increase in their wrong-doings to wander blindly.*❩-(Surah Al-Baqarah: 15). As lastly, it should be known that Allaah has commanded that the Muslims attach ourselves clearly to the believers, ❨*O you who believe! Be afraid of Allaah, and be with those who are true (in words and deeds)*❩-(Surah Al-Tawbah: 119) []

SHEIKH MUHAMMAD 'ALEE FERKOUS, MAY ALLAAH PRESERVE HIM

Sheikh Muhammad 'Alee Ferkous stated about secularism, [5] .

"....This is secularism which is currently spread throughout the Muslim world and the Arab lands as a result of colonialism, campaigns from Christian countries, direct evangelical efforts, and the gross heedlessness of those who have been enticed and beguiled from among the people of our own Muslim lands and origins who have elevated its false slogans and calls, those who have executed the conceived plans and goals of the disbelievers. It is supported by those same individuals who have beautified for acceptance by the common people, it's many misconceptions and false claims which stand at the height of misguidance. Some of that which they base their call upon is embodied within the following assertions:

- Their criticism and speaking against the Noble Qur'aan, as well as undermining and causing people to doubt the validity of affirming the belief that Allaah sent prophets with perfect revealed guidance.

---

[5] Secularism: Its Reality and Danger http://ferkous.com/home/?q=art-mois-13

- Their assertion that the Sharee'ah is by nature stagnant, and wholly incompatible with modern age and civilization. They state that Europe did truly start to progress until it wisely turned away from and minimized the influence of religion.

- Their claim that Islaam has failed to embrace evolutionary theories of the development of life, and instead calls to persecute and oppose absolute freedom of philosophical and scientific thought.

- Their claim that the religion of Islaam has already fulfilled its essential aims and original goals, and that nothing really remains of value within it other than a collection of rituals and spiritual practices.

- Their claim that the Arabic language has fallen behind and failed to contribute to modern corpus of knowledge and areas of contemporary advancement, and that the Arabic language is incapable of proceeding and moving forward with those intellectual mechanisms leading to modern progression and development. They assert that regardless of whether or not the Arabic language is the primary or main language in the Arab lands, that it is only marginally used in the majority of western administrative institutions, western universities, and western medical institutions specifically. As such it cannot be considered suitable for our true progress. They call for the French language to take the place of Arabic as the language used for conversation and essential standard for functional communication in the different spheres of life. They also call for the gradual withdrawal and abandonment the Arabic language, according to a calculated and deliberate strategy, due to their knowledge that it is indeed the language of the Qur'aan and that understanding Arabic is the key to understanding the various branches of Sharee'ah knowledge.

- They claim that the Sharee'ah is really only something implemented outwardly or superficially in governance, judicial rulings, and the other areas of societal life anyway. Additionally, as they falsely claim, most Islamic rulings are actually derived from or based on Roman Law in any case.

- They claim that the Sharee'ah is oppressive and harsh in its legislated corporal punishments related to criminal justice, the cutting of limbs, and the practice of stoning. They assert that more appropriate punishments must be adopted. This would be brought about by firstly adopting the religious systems and spiritual orientations from present Western civilizations and emulating them in order that criminal punishments be changed to be more merciful and reflect greater compassion.

These are the general assertions which the people of secularism hold to be true and employ in their efforts to negate the Sharee'ah of Allaah, the Most High. That effort is undertaken through various different methods and means, such as through specific prominent individuals, magazines, newspapers, and other means of promoting their ideas. This is all towards the greater goal of stripping the clear religion of *Hanafeeyah*, the worship of Allaah alone, out of the active life in Muslim societies through their false accusations against it, while also pushing for limitations on implementing of religion and restricting the boundaries, scope, and spheres of interaction in Muslim societies.

These people blindly follow the West in what Western societies have adopted and currently practice, towards the objective of removing the bonds and institutions of Islaam, encouraging the discarding of what Islaam advocates and it being actually implemented and established by Muslims, as well is striving to transform Muslim identity. The goal or object intended for the Muslims is the severing of their relationship with Islaam and removing their allegiance towards the religion, as well as their connection and attribution to their Muslim Ummah- by developing and fostering a blind allegiance and love of Western societies and their malicious interests among Muslims.

Since Islaam is both a way of life and a system of governance, it rejects this separation or the establishing of an unpassable barrier in human life between the worlds of our material interests and physical well-being from the world of our spiritual interests and true everlasting existence; with an absolute definitive rejection. Islaam considers knowingly affirming this devised separation as apostasy from Islaam. Likewise Islaam in its purity and soundness, the clarity of its beliefs, and its excellent character cannot accept what has spread of many societal problems and illnesses within Western society which are the results of disbelieving secularism, as well as the spreading of unrestrained sexual licentiousness, unprecedented chaos in people's personalities and characters, personal vices, and filthy disgraceful beliefs and character traits. These matters along with the dangerous fragmentation of the structure of both the family and society as a whole in western countries are all eventual consequences of the tearing down of the essential belief of Allaah's right to be worshiped alone.

Rather, Islaam commands the Muslim to surrender himself and make every single sphere of his life solely for the sake of Allaah alone. By this meaning that his actions and statements, his behavior and conduct, his living in and his dying, all become something done for the sake of Allaah the Most Perfect and the Most High, as it is found in the Qur'aan ❁*Say (O Muhammad): "Verily, my Salaat (prayer), my sacrifice, my living, and my dying are for Allaah, the Lord of the 'Alameen (mankind, jinn and all that exists). He has no partner. And of this I have been commanded, and I am the first of the Muslims.*❁ -(Surah Al-An'am: 162-163)

May Allaah's praise and salutation be upon Muhammad and upon his family, and his Companions, and his brothers until the day of reckoning

Sheikh Muhammad Ibn Saaleh al-'Utheimeen, May Allaah Have Mercy Upon Him

Sheikh Muhammad Ibn Saaleh al-'Utheimeen, may Allaah have mercy upon him, was asked, [6]

"What is the ruling on interpreting the meaning of the hadeeth, referring to the hadeeth describing the callers to doors to Hellfire upon the false paths, to mean that those callers are the secularists we find today?"

The sheikh replied: "What I hold to be correct is that what is intended in the narration is general, applying both to the secularist as well as to others upon misguidance, such that the Jahmeeyah, the Mu'tazilah, and others who also fall within this description, of inviters at the doors of Hellfire."

He was also asked[7]: *"Is it permissible for the student of knowledge who is well grounded in Sharee'ah knowledge to engage in dialogues with the people who adhere to their personal desires in fundamental beliefs, such as the secularists and others in order to publicly clarify their doubts and misconceptions and refute their false claims and assertions about the religion of Islaam?"*

Sheikh Al-'Utheimeen says: "Are you asking if this is permissible?"

Questioner: Yes.

The Sheikh replied: "I say and hold that it is obligatory, in fact obligatory upon those well-grounded students that they engage in dialogues with these individuals, in conformance with the statement of Allaah the Most High,

[6] Found questions answered during lessons in the sheik's explanation of Saheeh Muslim, Kitab al-Jihaad
[7] Open Door Gatherings No. 235

❦Invite (mankind, O Muhammad) to the Way of your Lord (i.e. Islaam) with wisdom (i.e. with the Divine Inspiration and the Qur'aan) and fair preaching, and argue with them in a way that is better. ❦-(Surah An-Nahl:125) Additionally, if you sufficiently clarify the truth to them, yet these people refuse to recant and repent from their false claims, then it is upon the governmental authority to compel them to abandon those claims, or that the authorities mandate for these secularists discretionary judicial punishments which will deter them from advocating this call to falsehood.

Because it is not in any way acceptable that we leave these misguided people and their Shaytaans free, unrestricted, and unaccountable to say whatever they wish of falsehood within society, while we, all praise is due to Allaah, still possess the ability, the control, and the authority to prevent this. As such, it is required that we restrain these secularists in order that their corruption not spread through the earth. Consider case of the one whose transgression and harm in society reaches the level of seizing people's wealth. The ruling of the religion in this situation is well known, *❦The recompense of those who wage war against Allaah and His Messenger and do mischief in the land is only that they shall be killed or crucified or their hands and their feet be cut off on the opposite sides, or be exiled from the land. That is their disgrace in this world, and a great torment is theirs in the Hereafter. ❦*-(Surah Al-Ma'idah:33). If this is the case of these transgressing people who illegally steal and seize the wealth of people and attack their physical lives, then what of the more severe situation of those who in fact strip away the people's very religion away from them, denying them both success and goodness in this world as well as the next life!?!

For the case of the disbeliever is that he is a loser in relation to both this world as well as the final situation in the hereafter. How is this so? In this world, every day passes never to return, isn't that the case? And what did they, the disbelievers, benefit from it? What did they benefit from that day which permanently passed away? They didn't truly benefit anything of true worth. Even if they reach the highest and most intense of physical pleasures, then that also passes and doesn't really benefit them. That day itself ends and passes, and so does the next, and so forth until a person dies. In this way they are clearly the losers in both.

As in the Hereafter are they also considered losers or not. Definitely losers! Allaah says, ❴*The losers are those who will lose themselves and their families on the Day of Resurrection. Verily, that will be a manifest loss!*❵-(Surah Az-Zumar:15). So consider that these secularists are people who invite and call people to embrace clear disbelief and atheism which means that what they want from the people to embrace something which actually destroys both their success in this life as well as their success in the next life. So which of these two is the greater form of corruption? These secularists or those criminals who steal and seize people's wealth and violently attack and kill people? Certainly, the secularists are greater and more significant in the harm they lead to since the good of both lives, this world and the next, is lost. Due to this we clearly warn against this ideological colonization, and this colonization of both the social character and the Islamic way of life which the enemies of the Muslim Ummah have planted and spread today through the means such as of satellite channels, the internet, and forms of media that are similar to these.

At present, these enemies are not able to successfully defeat the Muslim Ummah militarily due to our position and circumstances, and all praise is due to Allaah. However they have instead attacked us ideologically, and attacked our Muslim character and the very understanding of the Muslims by spreading doubts and misconceptions among us. As when they find a Muslim state and society weak then they usually seek to dominate it through military means, isn't this the case?

Consider and look at the situation in Chechnya and other Muslim regions. Due to this, it is a requirement upon us, as Muslims, that we think and consider this matter and situation very well, closely, and in great detail. At the very least, we must fortify and strengthen ourselves from the onslaught of the ideological diseases that are directed against us.

Oh Allaah, preserve for us our religion, and make us steadfast upon it until death. Strengthen our national leaders in their opposition to our enemies' efforts. Bless them with a fortification that protects and strengthens them in the face of evil and corruption confronting them.

Our time to speak has ended. And all praise is due to Allaah the Lord of all the Worlds, may Allaah's praise and salutation be upon our Prophet Muhammad and his family, and all his Companions. May Allaah grant us success, and assist us and you in all our affairs."

THE NAKHLAH EDUCATIONAL SERIES:

MISSION

The Purpose of the 'Nakhlah Educational Series' is to contribute to the present knowledge based efforts which enable Muslim individuals, families, and communities to understand and learn Islaam and then to develop within and truly live Islaam. Our commitment and goal is to contribute beneficial publications and works that:

Firstly, reflect the priority, message and methodology of all the prophets and messengers sent to humanity, meaning that single revealed message which embodies the very purpose of life, and of human creation. As Allaah the Most High has said,

◈ *We sent a Messenger to every nation ordering them that they should worship Allaah alone, obey Him and make their worship purely for Him, and that they should avoid everything worshipped besides Allaah. So from them there were those whom Allaah guided to His religion, and there were those who were unbelievers for whom misguidance was ordained. So travel through the land and see the destruction that befell those who denied the Messengers and disbelieved.* ◈ —(Surah an-Nahl: 36)

Two Essential Foundations

Secondly, building upon the above foundation, our commitment is to contributing publications and works which reflect the inherited message and methodology of the acknowledged scholars of the many various branches of Sharee'ah knowledge who stood upon the straight path of preserved guidance in every century and time since the time of our Messenger, may Allaah's praise and salutations be upon him. These people of knowledge, who are the inheritors of the Final Messenger, have always adhered closely to the two revealed sources of guidance: the Book of Allaah and the Sunnah of the Messenger of Allaah- may Allaah's praise and salutations be upon him, upon the united consensus, standing with the body of guided Muslims in every century - preserving and transmitting the true religion generation after generation. Indeed the Messenger of Allaah, may Allaah's praise and salutations be upon him, informed us that, *{ A group of people amongst my Ummah will remain obedient to Allaah's orders. They will not be harmed by those who leave them nor by those who oppose them, until Allaah's command for the Last Day comes upon them while they remain on the right path. }* (Authentically narrated in Saheeh al-Bukhaaree).

The guiding scholar Sheikh Zayd al-Madkhalee, may Allaah protect him, stated in his writing, 'The Well Established Principles of the Way of the First Generations of Muslims: It's Enduring & Excellent Distinct Characteristics' that,

"From among these principles and characteristics is that the methodology of tasfeeyah -or clarification, and tarbeeyah -or education and cultivation- is clearly affirmed and established as a true way coming from the first three generations of Islaam, and is something well known to the people of true merit from among them, as is concluded by considering all the related evidence.

What is intended by tasfeeyah, when referring to it generally, is clarifying that which is the truth from that which is falsehood, what is goodness from that which is harmful and corrupt, and when referring to its specific meanings it is distinguishing the noble Sunnah of the Prophet and the people of the Sunnah from those innovated matters brought into the religion and the people who are supporters of such innovations.

As for what is intended by tarbeeyah, it is calling all of the creation to take on the manners and embrace the excellent character invited to by that guidance revealed to them by their Lord through His worshiper and Messenger Muhammad, may Allaah's praise and salutations be upon him; so that they might have good character, manners, and behavior. As without this they cannot have a good life, nor can they put right their present condition or their final destination. And we seek refuge in Allaah from the evil of not being able to achieve that rectification."

Thus the methodology of the people of standing upon the Prophet's Sunnah, and proceeding upon the 'way of the believers' in every century is reflected in a focus and concern with these two essential matters: tasfeeyah or clarification of what is original, revealed message from the Lord of all the worlds, and tarbeeyah or education and raising of ourselves, our families, and our communities, and our lands upon what has been distinguished to be that true message and path.

METHODOLOGY:

The Roles of the Scholars & General Muslims In Raising the New Generation

The priority and focus of the 'Nakhlah Educational Series' is reflected within in the following statements of Sheikh al-Albaanee, may Allaah have mercy upon him:

"As for the other obligation, then I intend by this the education of the young generation upon Islaam purified from all of those impurities we have mentioned, giving them a correct Islamic education from their very earliest years, without any influence of a foreign, disbelieving education."

(Silsilat al-Hadeeth ad-Da'eefah, Introduction page 2.)

"...And since the Messenger of Allaah, may Allaah's praise and salutations be upon him, has indicated that the only cure to remove this state of humiliation that we find ourselves entrenched within, is truly returning back to the religion. Then it is clearly obligatory upon us - through the people of knowledge- to correctly and properly understand the religion in a way that conforms to the sources of the Book of Allaah and the Sunnah, and that we educate and raise a new virtuous, righteous generation upon this."

(Clarification and Cultivation and the Need of the Muslims for Them)

It is essential in discussing our perspective upon this obligation of raising the new generation of Muslims, that we highlight and bring attention to a required pillar of these efforts as indicated by Sheikh al-Albaanee, may Allaah have mercy upon him, and others- in the golden words, "*through the people of knowledge*". Since something we commonly experience today is that many people have various incorrect understandings of the role that the scholars should have in the life of a Muslim, failing to understand the way in which they fulfill their position as the inheritors of the Messenger of Allaah, may Allaah's praise and salutations be upon him, and stand as those who preserve and enable us to practice the guidance of Islaam.

Similarly the guiding scholar Sheikh 'Abdul-'Azeez Ibn Baaz, may Allaah have mercy upon him, also emphasized this same overall responsibility:

"...It is also upon a Muslim that he struggles diligently in that which will place his worldly affairs in a good state, just as he must also strive in the correcting of his religious affairs and the affairs of his own family. As the people of his household have a significant right over him that he strive diligently in rectifying their affair and guiding them towards goodness, due to the statement of Allaah, the Most Exalted, ❧ ***Oh you who believe! Save yourselves and your families Hellfire whose fuel is men and stones*** ❧ *-(Surah at-Tahreem: 6)*

So it is upon you to strive to correct the affairs of the members of your family. This includes your wife, your children- both male and female- and such as your own brothers. This concerns all of the people in your family, meaning you should strive to teach them the religion, guiding and directing them, and warning them from those matters Allaah has prohibited for us. Because you are the one who is responsible for them as shown in the statement of the Prophet, may Allaah's praise and salutations be upon him, **{ *Every one of you is a guardian,*** *and responsible for what is in his custody. The ruler is a guardian of his subjects and responsible for them; a husband is a guardian of his family and is responsible for it; a lady is a guardian of her husband's house and is responsible for it, and a servant is a guardian of his master's property and is responsible for it....}* Then the Messenger of Allaah, may Allaah's praise and salutations be upon him, continued to say, *{...so all of you are guardians and are responsible for those under your authority.} (Authentically narrated in Saheeh al-Bukhaaree & Muslim)*

It is upon us to strive diligently in correcting the affairs of the members of our families, from the aspect of purifying their sincerity of intention for Allaah's sake alone in all of their deeds, and ensuring that they truthfully believe in and follow the Messenger of Allaah, may Allaah's praise and salutations be upon him, their fulfilling the prayer and the other obligations which Allaah the Most Exalted has commanded for us, as well as from the direction of distancing them from everything which Allaah has prohibited.

It is upon every single man and women to give advice to their families about the fulfillment of what is obligatory upon them. Certainly, it is upon the woman as well as upon the man to perform this. In this way our homes become corrected and rectified in regard to the most important and essential matters. Allaah said to His Prophet, may Allaah's praise and salutations be upon him, ❧ ***And enjoin the ritual prayers on your family...*** ❧ *(Surah Taha: 132) Similarly, Allaah the Most Exalted said to His prophet Ismaa'aeel,* ❧ ***And mention in the Book, Ismaa'aeel. Verily, he was true to what he promised, and he was a Messenger, and a Prophet. And he used to enjoin on his family and his people the ritual prayers and the obligatory charity, and his Lord was pleased with him.*** ❧
-(Surah Maryam: 54-55)

As such, it is only proper that we model ourselves after the prophets and the best of people, and be concerned with the state of the members of our households. Do not be neglectful of them, oh worshipper of Allaah! Regardless of whether it is concerning your wife, your mother, father, grandfather, grandmother, your brothers, or your children; it is upon you to strive diligently in correcting their state and condition..."

(Collection of Various Rulings and Statements- Sheikh 'Abdul-'Azeez Ibn 'Abdullah Ibn Baaz, Vol. 6, page 47)

Content & Structure:

We hope to contribute works which enable every striving Muslim who acknowledges the proper position of the scholars, to fulfill the recognized duty and obligation which lays upon each one of us to bring the light of Islaam into our own lives as individuals as well as into our homes and among our families. Towards this goal we are committed to developing educational publications and comprehensive educational curriculums -through cooperation with and based upon the works of the scholars of Islaam and the students of knowledge. Works which, with the assistance of Allaah, the Most High, we can utilize to educate and instruct ourselves, our families and our communities upon Islaam in both principle and practice. The publications and works of the Nakhlah Educational Series are divided into the following categories:

Basic: Ages 4- 6

Elementary: Ages 6-11

Secondary: Ages 11-14

High School: Ages 14- Young Adult

General: Young Adult –Adult

Supplementary: All Ages

Publications and works within these stated levels will, with the permission of Allaah, encompass different beneficial areas and subjects, and will be offered in every permissible form of media and medium. As certainly, as the guiding scholar Sheikh Saaleh Fauzaan al-Fauzaan, may Allaah preserve him, has stated,

"Beneficial knowledge is itself divided into two categories. Firstly is that knowledge which is tremendous in its benefit, as it benefits in this world and continues to benefit in the Hereafter. This is religious Sharee'ah knowledge. And secondly, that which is limited and restricted to matters related to the life of this world, such as learning the processes of manufacturing various goods. This is a category of knowledge related specifically to worldly affairs.

...As for the learning of worldly knowledge, such as knowledge of manufacturing, then it is legislated upon us collectively to learn whatever the Muslims have a need for. Yet If they do not have a need for this knowledge, then learning it is a neutral matter upon the condition that it does not compete with or displace any areas of Sharee'ah knowledge..."

("Explanations of the Mistakes of Some Writers'", Pages 10-12)

We ask Allaah, the most High to bless us with success in contributing to the many efforts of our Muslim brothers and sisters committed to raising themselves as individuals and the next generation of our children upon that Islaam which Allaah has perfected and chosen for us, and which He has enabled the guided Muslims to proceed upon in each and every century. We ask him to forgive us, and forgive the Muslim men and the Muslim women, and to guide all the believers to everything He loves and is pleased with. The success is from Allaah, The Most High The Most Exalted, alone and all praise is due to Him.

Abu Sukhailah Khalil Ibn-Abelahyi
Taalib al-Ilm Educational Resources

BOOK PUBLICATION PREVIEW:

30 Days of Guidance:
Cultivating The Character & Behavior of Islaam

A Short Journey within the Work al-Adab al-Mufrad with
Sheikh Zayd Ibn Haadee al-Madhkhaalee

(may Allaah have mercy on him)

This book is intended for the Muslim individual for self-study, for us as Muslim parents in our essential efforts to educate our children within Islaam and our ongoing endeavor of cultivating them upon the extraordinary character and behavior of our beloved Prophet, may the praise and salutations of Allaah be upon him. It is also intended to be an easy to use classroom resource for our Muslim teachers in the every growing numbers of Islamic centers, masjids, and Islamic weekend and full-time schools.

Divided into 30 daily selections of one or more related authentic narrations, it has brief explanations and practical discussions on implementing their guidance in our lives from the well known scholar: Sheikh Zayd Ibn Muhammad Ibn Haadee, may Allaah have mercy upon him.

Compiled and Translated by:
Abu Sukhailah Khalil Ibn-Abelahyi

[Available: **Now** ¦ **(SS) $27.50 (DS) $25 (W) $12** ¦ **(Kindle) $9.99**]

BOOK PUBLICATION PREVIEW:

30 Days of Guidance:
Learning Fundamental Principles of Islaam

A Short Journey Within the Work al-Ibanah al-Sughrah With
Sheikh 'Abdul-Azeez Ibn 'Abdullah ar-Raajihee
(may Allaah preserve him)

The role of Islaam in today's world is something which is indisputable. Yet there are many different understanding of Islaam from range from dangerous extremism all the way to dangerous laxity which nullifies most beliefs and practices of revealed guidance.

For every Muslim who wishes to live their life in a way pleasing to Allaah it is essential that they ensure that their beliefs and practices actually have evidence and support from within the sources of Islaam. This book approaches this challenge in a way that allows an individual to proceed through discussions related to this- a day at a time over thirty days- based upon the explanation of one of today's steadfast noble scholars.

Compiled and Translated by:
Abu Sukhailah Khalil Ibn-Abelahyi

[Available: **Now** ¦ **(SS)** $27.50 **(DS)** $25 **(W)** $12 ¦ **(Kindle) $9.99**]

BOOK PUBLICATION PREVIEW:

An Educational Course Based Upon: Beneficial Answers to Questions On Innovated Methodologies

By the Guiding Scholar
Sheikh Saaleh Ibn Abdullah al-Fauzaan
(may Allaah preserve him)

This course focuses upon the importance of clarity, in the midst of today's confusion, in the way you understand and practice Islaam. But what is the right way or methodology to do so? Examine the evidences and proofs from the sources texts of the Qur'aan and Sunnah and the statements of many scholars explaining them, that connect you directly to the Islaam which the Messenger of Allaah ﷺ taught his Companions, may Allaah be pleased with them all.

Course Features:

Consists of 20 short lessons to facilitate learning and review with several important textual and course appendixes.

Compiled and Translated by:
Abu Sukhailah Khalil Ibn-Abelahyi

[Available: **Now** ¦ pages: 450+ ¦ price: (S) **$30** (H) **$40** ¦ eBook **$9.99**]

BOOK PUBLICATION PREVIEW:

Lessons & Benefits From the Two Excellent Works:
The Belief of Every Muslim & The Methodology of The Saved Sect

By the Guiding Scholar
Sheikh Muhammad Ibn Jameel Zaynoo
(may Allaah preserve him)

[Self Study/Teachers Edition] Book 1

Course Features:

This course begins with three full lessons with specific practical guidelines on how to effectively study Islaam and gain the knowledge needed to build your life as a Muslim into that which is pleasing to Allaah.

Through twenty lessons on knowledge, beliefs, & methodology along with quizzes, review questions & lesson benefits., the remaining lessons cover several important principles, and the common misconceptions connected to them, which are fundamental to correctly understanding Islaam as it was taught to the Companions of the Messenger of Allaah.

Compiled and Translated by:
Abu Sukhailah Khalil Ibn-Abelahyi

[Available: **Now** | pages: 370+ | price: (S) **$30** (H) **$40** | eBook **$9.99**]

BOOK PREVIEW

BOOK PUBLICATION PREVIEW:
Statements of the Guiding Scholars of Our Age Regarding Books & their Advice to the Beginner Seeker of Knowledge

with Selections from the Following Scholars:
Sheikh 'Abdul-'Azeez ibn 'Abdullah ibn Baaz - Sheikh Muhammad ibn Saaleh al-'Utheimein - Sheikh Muhammad Naasiruddeen al-Albaanee - Sheikh Muqbil ibn Haadee al-Waada'ee - Sheikh 'Abdur-Rahman ibn Naaser as-Sa'adee - Sheikh Muhammad 'Amaan al-Jaamee - Sheikh Muhammad al-Ameen as-Shanqeetee - Sheikh Ahmad ibn Yahya an-Najmee & Sheikh Saaleh al-Fauzaan ibn 'Abdullah al-Fauzaan - Sheikh Saaleh ibn 'Abdul-'Azeez Aal-Sheikh - Sheikh Muhammad ibn 'Abdul-Wahhab al-Wasaabee - Permanent Committee to Scholastic Research & Issuing Of Islamic Rulings

With an introduction by: Sheikh Muhammad Ibn 'Abdullah al-Imaam
Collected and Translated by Abu Sukhailah Khalil Ibn-Abelahyi al-Amreekee

[Available: **Now** | pages: 370+ | price: (S) **$25** (H) **$32** | eBook **$9.99**]

BOOK PUBLICATION PREVIEW:

Al-Waajibaat:
The Obligatory Matters

What it is Decreed that Every Male and Female Muslim Must Have Knowledge Of -from the statements of Sheikh al-Islaam Muhammad ibn 'Abdul-Wahaab

(A Step By Step Course on The Fundamental Beliefs of Islaam- with Lesson Questions, Quizzes, & Exams)

Collected and Arranged by
Umm Mujaahid Khadijah Bint Lacina
al-Amreekiyyah

[Available: **Now** - **Self Study/ Teachers Edition**
price: (Soft cover) **$20** (Hard cover) **$27**
Directed Study Edition price: **$17.50** -
Exercise Workbook price: **$10** ¦ eBook **$9.99**]

BOOK PUBLICATION PREVIEW:

Fasting from Alif to Yaa:
A Day by Day Guide to Making the Most of Ramadhaan

-Contains additional points of benefit to teach one how to live Islaam as a way of life
-Plus, stories of the Prophets and Messengers including activities for the whole family to enjoy and benefit from for each day of Ramadhaan. Some of the Prophets and Messengers covered include Aadam, Ibraaheem, Lut, Yusuf, Sulaymaan, Shu'ayb, Moosa, Zakariyyah, Muhammad, and more!
-Recipes for foods enjoyed by Muslims around the world

By Umm Mujaahid Khadijah Bint Lacina al-Amreekiyyah as-Salafiyyah With Abu Hamzah Hudhaifah Ibn Khalil and Umm Usaamah Sukhailah Bint Khalil

{Available: **1433** -pages: 250+ | price: (S) **$20** (H) **$27** | eBook **$9.99**

SCAN WITH SMARTPHONE — PRINT — FOR MORE INFORMATION

SCAN WITH SMARTPHONE — EBOOK — FOR MORE INFORMATION

BOOK PREVIEW

BOOK PUBLICATION PREVIEW:

A Lighthouse of Knowledge From A Guardian of the Sunnah:

Sheikh Rabee'a Ibn Haadee 'Umair al-Madkhalee
[Books 1 & 2]

Book 1: Unity, Advice, Brotherhood & the Call to Allaah
Book 2: The Connection with the People of Knowledge, Affairs of Brotherhood & Other Benefits

Collected and Translated by
Abu Sukhailah Khalil Ibn-Abelahyi al-Amreekee

[Available: **Now**¦ pages: **380+** ¦ price: (Soft cover) **$20** (Hard cover) **$27** eBook **$9.99**]

BOOK PUBLICATION PREVIEW:

My Hijaab, My Path

A Comprehensive Knowledge Based Compilation on Muslim Women's Role & Dress

*Collected and Translated by
Umm Mujaahid Khadijah Bint Lacina
al-Amreekiyyah*

[Available: **Now**¦ pages: **190+** ¦ price: (S) **$17.50**
(H) **$25** ¦ eBook **$9.99**

BOOK PUBLICATION PREVIEW:

My Home, My Path

A Comprehensive Source Book For Today's Muslim Woman Discussing Her Essential Role & Contribution To The Establishment of Islaam – Taken From The Words Of The People Of Knowledge

*Collected and Translated by
Umm Mujaahid Khadijah Bint Lacina
al-Amreekiyyah*

[Available: **Now**¦ pages: **420+** ¦ price: (Soft cover) **$25**
(Hard cover) **$35** (eBook) **$9.99**]

SCAN WITH SMARTPHONE
PRINT
FOR MORE INFORMATION

SCAN WITH SMARTPHONE
EBOOK
FOR MORE INFORMATION

BOOK PUBLICATION PREVIEW:

Thalaathatul-Usool: The Three Fundamental Principles

A Step by Step Educational Course on Islaam Based upon Commentaries of 'Thalaathatul-Usool' of Sheikh Muhammad ibn 'Abdul Wahaab (may Allaah have mercy upon him)

Collected and Arranged by Umm Mujaahid Khadijah Bint Lacina al-Amreekiyyah

Description:

A complete course for the Believing men and women who want to learn their religion from the ground up, building a firm foundation upon which to base their actions. This is the **second** *in our* **Foundation Series** *on Islamic beliefs and making them a reality in your life, which began with* **"al-Waajibaat: The Obligatory Matters"**.

[Available: **Now Self Study/ Teachers Edition** |
price: (Soft cover) **$27.50** (Hard cover) **$35**
Directed Study Edition price: (S) **$22.50** -
Exercise Workbook price: (S) **$12** | eBook **$9.99**]

BOOK PREVIEW

BOOK PUBLICATION PREVIEW:
The Cure, The Explanation, The Clear Affair, & The Brilliantly Distinct Signpost

A Step by Step Educational Course on Islaam Based upon Commentaries of

'Usul as-Sunnah' of Imaam Ahmad
(may Allaah have mercy upon him)

Study of text divided into chapters formatted into multiple short lessons to facilitate learning. Each lesson has: evidence summary, lesson benefits, standard & review exercises 'Usul as-Sunnah' Arabic text & translation divided for easier memorization.

Compiled and Translated by:
Abu Sukhailah Khalil Ibn-Abelahyi

[Available: **TBA** ¦ price: **TBA** (Multi-volume) ¦ soft cover, hard cover, ebook]

BOOK PUBLICATION PREVIEW:

Whispers of Paradise (1): A Muslim Woman's Life Journal

An Islamic Daily Journal Which Encourages Reflection & Rectification

Collected and Edited by Taalib al-Ilm Educational Resources Development Staff

[Available: **Now** ¦ price: (Soft cover) **$25**]

[New elegantly designed edition is for the year 1438 / 2017]

12 Monthly calendar pages with beneficial quotations from Ibn Qayyim
Daily journal page based upon Islamic calendar (with corresponding C.E. dates)

SCAN WITH SMARTPHONE

FOR MORE INFORMATION

www.ingramcontent.com/pod-product-compliance
Lightning Source LLC
Chambersburg PA
CBHW051655040426
42446CB00009B/1146